Faithful Women Who Built Nations by Building Homes

"We will tell the next generation the praiseworthy deeds of the Lord, His power, and the wonders He has done."
— PSALM 78:4

WRITTEN AND COMPILED BY
JEN THOMPSON
CO-FOUNDERS OF SMORES AND STRIPES
CO-CREATORS OF THE UNDER GOD PROJECT

Published by The Under God Project Press Dallas, Texas
© 2025 Jen Thompson. All rights reserved.

No portion of this publication may be reproduced or transmitted in any form or by any means without prior written permission of the publisher.

Dedication

To my daughters
    that you may know what God expects of you,
    and who you already are in His eyes.
    May these pages teach you to
    walk closely with our Father,
    to love His Word,
    and to see yourselves in the
    courageous and faithful women
    who came before you.

    When the world grows loud,
    listen for His still, steady voice.
    When the path feels uncertain,
    remember the strength,
    the gentleness,
    and the faith of the women
    who trusted Him first.

    You were created for this generation
    to be light, to be truth, and to be love.
    Grow in wisdom, in grace,
    and in the fearless joy of belonging to God.
    And when life calls you to stand firm,
    may you do so with a heart like Ruth's,
    a voice like Deborah's,
    and a spirit like Mary's
    undaunted, devoted, and deeply loved.

Know that your Father in Heaven
    sees you, calls you, and delights in you.

Mom

AN AMERICAN FAMILY PROMISE

Across the nation, families are rising to restore what was once the foundation of every strong home—faith, unity, and covenant.
The Family Under God Compact is a written promise between family members and their Creator, a renewal of the sacred order of home. It invites every household to pause, pray, and declare again that we are one family—under God.

This covenant began in our home as a way to bring our family before the Lord together, but it has since become a nationwide movement. From kitchen tables to church pews, families in every state are adopting the Compact, adding their names, and joining hands across America to rebuild the moral and spiritual fabric of our nation—one household at a time.

Through UnderGodProject.com, families can read, adopt, and share their own Compact. Each signed promise joins a growing network of homes committed to living by God's design: where parents lead in love, children are nurtured in faith, and every member is valued as part of His divine story.

This devotional, A Biblical Woman, flows from the same covenant heart. Just as the Compact calls families to unity, this book calls women to purpose—to rediscover the sacred strength, gentleness, and faith that keep the light of the home burning.

When a woman walks in covenant with God, she shapes more than her household—she strengthens her nation.
When families align their lives with His Word, the story of America becomes what it was always meant to be: a living testimony of faith and freedom.

We invite you to join us in this covenant renewal. Visit UnderGodProject.com to adopt the Compact, share your family's promise, and stand among those choosing to live as One Nation Under God Again.

OUR FAMILY UNDER GOD

A Promise

We are the {...} family, and on this {...} day of {Month}, of, {year} we declare that we are One Family Under God.

We believe that it is our right and our privilege to glorify God, and to enjoy and give thanks for what He has given us, especially for one another. The story of our faith is a story of the creation, sanctification, and preservation of families, and the story of our family is a continuation of the divine story.

We believe that God created families, and therefore the family is sacred and ordained by God. We believe that our family was created specifically for this time.

We know that every father and mother before us has led directly to our family today, and we believe they have been placed in our history so that we could be brought together.

As a family we pledge to love one another, to be a light to each other and the world around us. We pledge to learn more about our family history, and to learn and instruct our children on how best to honor God with our time, our talents, and our treasures.

As parents, we believe that our children are a gift from God, and our highest responsibility on earth.

As children, we believe that we are given the opportunity to learn from our fathers and mothers, and theirs before them, how to live an abundant and fulfilling life by honoring God and our parents.

We believe we are always essential to each other, essential to God's family, our extended family on earth.

We know that though there may be prodigals, or in pain, or wandering for a time, and while some of us may have been lost, we are still a family created by God. All of us were once prodigals to God, yet never abandoned or lost to Him, so we commit to never abandon those he has given to us.

We pledge to strengthen our faith and family ties, to uplift and encourage one another, and to stand firm in the face of any effort within or without to dim our light, love, or liberty to one another.

To that end we promise together as a family to continually: {personal family promises}

May God give us patience, strength, and peace as we keep these promises to one another, and may

God bless
THIS AMERICAN FAMILY.
In the Name of God,
Amen.

A BIBLICAL WOMAN

DAY 1

Ruth

Faithfulness: The Beauty of Faithfullness

The sun shimmered across the dusty road, wrapping the hills near Bethlehem in a golden haze. Naomi walked slowly, her heart heavy from loss, each step stirring the memories of the husband and sons she had buried in Moab. Beside her walked Ruth, quiet, steady, her eyes full of promise and faith.
Naomi urged her to turn back. "My daughter, go home. Return to your people, to your gods, to the chance of another life." Orpah kissed her mother-in-law and wept, retreating toward what was familiar. But Ruth stood firm, her voice strong and certain, a melody of covenant and devotion: "Where you go, I will go. Where you lodge, I will lodge. Your people shall be my people, and your God my God." Ruth 1:16
Those words were not simply a promise—they were a vow of love and faith. In that moment, Ruth's heart anchored to Naomi's, and even more deeply to the heart of God. When the barley fields ripened under the spring sun, Ruth's faithfulness took shape in humble, holy work. She rose with the dawn, hands gathering grain beneath the heat of the day, her brow glistening with effort and grace. Every kernel gleaned was an act of trust, believing that God would take her "not enough" and turn it into abundance.
And He did.
 Boaz saw her, saw the beauty of her loyalty, the quiet strength of her devotion—and spoke blessing over her:
"The Lord repay you for what you have done."
 Ruth 2:12

Faithfulness may not glitter before men. It often looks like the small, hidden choices—a steady walk down a lonely road, or hands that keep working when no one notices. But heaven always sees.
Through Ruth's steadfast heart, God wove redemption itself.
 From her lineage came David, and through him, Christ—the Redeemer of all.

Reflection:

Faithfulness is covenant love, quietly lived out each day. It's the trust your husband rests in, the safety your children grow within, and the delight your Father finds in you. It doesn't seek applause, it simply endures, holding the home together with grace unseen.

Challenge:

Write a one-sentence family covenant
 ("In this house, we will _____ unto the Lord")
  and post it where all can see and remember.

Deeper Study:

Where has steadfast love carried our home through a hard season—and what beauty did it leave behind?

Prayer

"LORD, root me so deeply in Your faithfulness that peace fills my home, even in the storm."

Where has steadfast love carried our home through a hard season—and what beauty did it leave behind?

DAY 1: FAITHFULNESS: THE BEAUTY OF FAITHFULLNESS

A BIBLICAL WOMAN

DAY 2

Abigail

Wisdom: The Radiance of Wisdom

Evening shadows stretched long across the hills of Carmel as Abigail's servants hurried to load the donkeys, baskets of warm bread, figs glistening with honey, and roasted grain fragrant in the twilight. Beneath the calm bustle ran a pulse of urgency: David's men were on their way, swords drawn, vengeance burning hot.

Her husband, Nabal, had answered kindness with insult. And now, his folly endangered them all.

Abigail wasted no time. Cloak billowing behind her, she mounted her donkey and rode out into the wind, dust rising with each stride. Over the ridge, she saw them, hundreds of warriors, faces hard, eyes set. The setting sun caught their blades, a sea of fire and steel. She dismounted swiftly, lowering herself to the ground before David, not in fear, but in holy resolve. Her voice, steady and sure, broke through the tension:

"Upon me alone, my lord, be the guilt."

  1 Samuel 25:24

Then she spoke words of peace, of promise, reminding him that vengeance was the Lord's, not his. Her wisdom turned wrath aside like a gentle hand calming a storm.

David's heartbeat slowed. The fire in his eyes dimmed to awe.

"Blessed be the Lord... and blessed be your discretion."

  1 Samuel 25:32–33

Abigail's wisdom saved lives that night. Not by might, nor manipulation, but by truth spoken with grace.

Reflection:

Wisdom is not sharp cleverness—it is gentle discernment born of reverence for the Lord. She opens her mouth with kindness, and faithful instruction flows like honey (Prov 31:26; Jas 1:5). A wise woman speaks words that build, not words that burn. Her home becomes a sanctuary of peace because her voice carries heaven's tone

Challenge:

"Three Edifying Sentences" Today, speak life: One blessing to your husband. One blessing to each child. One blessing to yourself, rooted in God's Word. Let your tongue become a fountain of grace.

Deeper Study:

Proverbs 18:21 – Life and death are in the power of the tongue
James 1:19–20 – Quick to listen, slow to speak
Colossians 4:6 – Speech seasoned with grace

Prayer

"Spirit of God, fill my mouth with wisdom and my heart with peace. Let faithful instruction flow from my tongue, that every word I speak would plant life."

What words do I repeat that tear down or bring heaviness?
How can I replace them with Scripture that heals and uplifts?

Day 2: Wisdom: The Radiance of Wisdom

DAY 3

Jesus
Sacrifice: The Greatness of Hidden Work

The upper room was filled with the scent of roasted lamb and bitter herbs, the quiet clinking of clay cups, and the murmur of friends who loved Him yet could not grasp what the night would hold.

By the doorway sat a basin of cool water and a folded towel, waiting, as though creation itself held its breath. Dusty feet shuffled. No one moved.

Then Jesus rose.

Conversations faded. The Master, the One who calmed storms and called the dead to life, laid aside His robe, tied the towel around His waist, and poured water into the basin. The sound of the water was startling in its simplicity, a melody of humility.

Kneeling before each of them, He took their feet, calloused, dirt-streaked, weary from the road, and washed them with tenderness that only heaven could hold.

Peter flinched at the thought of such reversal. But Jesus looked up, eyes steady and full of love:

"If I do not wash you, you have no share with Me."
  John 13:8

When He had finished, He said softly,

"I have given you an example, that you also should do just as I have done to you."
  John 13:15

The Lord of Glory knelt with a towel.

 The hands that shaped galaxies washed the dust from tired feet.

 He showed that in the Kingdom of Heaven, greatness is not crowned, it kneels.

Hidden work is holy. Service is strength.

 And love, when poured out quietly, changes everything.

Reflection:

Service is not small; it is sacred.
> Jesus showed us that greatness wears a towel, not a crown (Mark 10:45). Hidden acts of love are heaven's language; quiet seeds that grow into eternal harvests. When we serve in secret, God Himself bears witness, and grace multiplies through our hands.

Challenge:

Choose one task your husband dislikes or overlooks, and do it with joy this week, unannounced, as worship. Let your heart smile in the doing, knowing heaven sees what others do not.

Deeper Study:

Mark 9:35 – The servant of all is greatest
> Colossians 3:23–24 – Work as unto the Lord
> Galatians 5:13 – Through love, serve one another

Prayer

"LORD Jesus, make my hands like Yours—strong and gentle, willing and pure. Teach me to serve with love that asks nothing in return, and to ind Your joy in the quiet work no one sees."

Which hidden task forms Christ in me the most?
How can I meet that place of service with deeper joy instead of duty?

Day 3: Sacrifice: The Greatness of Hidden Work

A Biblical Woman

DAY 4
Deborah

Strength: Clothed for the Day

The land trembled beneath the thunder of Sisera's iron chariots. Villages fell silent, fields grew wild, and fear crept through Israel like a long shadow. Yet under the shade of a palm tree near Ramah, a woman sat with quiet authority.

Her name was Deborah, a wife, a prophet, a mother in Israel.

People came from far and wide to seek her counsel, and her words—rooted in God, were like cool water in a dry land.

Then one day, the Lord's command stirred her spirit. She stood, strength rising like dawn within her, and declared:

"Up! For this is the day the Lord has given Sisera into your hand."

Judges 4:14

Storm clouds gathered. The Kishon River swelled, swallowing the chariots that once terrified the land. Soldiers scattered. And in a humble tent nearby, another woman, Jael, waited.

When Sisera stumbled into her tent, weary and desperate, she welcomed him with milk and a blanket, a mother's kindness concealing warrior courage. When he slept, she reached for the tools of her everyday world, a hammer and a tent peg, and, with steady hands, brought an end to Israel's oppression.

Strength took two forms that day: Deborah's fearless leadership and Jael's quiet resolve. Both were women clothed in courage, ready when God called.

Reflection:

Biblical strength is not loud or defiant, it is clothed in dignity, resolve, and obedience under pressure (Prov 31:25; Isa 40:31).
It is the kind of strength that stands tall in storms and bends low in surrender—courage wrapped in peace, anchored in trust.

Challenge:

Write a "strength verse" on your mirror, and speak it aloud morning and night for three days. Let it remind your heart that your power comes not from striving, but from standing, in joy, in steadiness, and in God's presence.

Deeper Study:

Joshua 1:9 – Be strong and courageous
Isaiah 40:29–31 – Strength renewed for those who wait on the Lord
2 Corinthians 12:9–10 – His power made perfect in weakness

Prayer

"LORD, clothe me in quiet strength. Arm me with joy, steadiness, and faith that does not waver. Let my courage flow from Your Spirit, and may my heart be fearless in obedience."

Where do I need courage to say yes—or no—this week?
What would it look like to answer with both firmness and grace?

Day 4: Strength: Clothed for the Day

A Biblical Woman

DAY 5

Mary

Joy: Setting the Atmosphere

The stone steps echoed softly as Mary climbed toward Zechariah's home, her hands resting over the new life stirring within her. The air smelled of olive oil and bread; her heart beat with quiet awe.
Inside, Elizabeth turned, and at the sound of Mary's greeting, her own child leapt for joy.
 Laughter filled the room, bright and full, joy tangible as sunlight dancing across the walls.
Elizabeth's voice rang out with blessing:
"Blessed are you among women, and blessed is the fruit of your womb!"
 Luke 1:42
Mary's eyes glistened. Her young soul swelled with reverent wonder, and then, like a spring bursting forth, she sang:
"My soul magnifies the Lord,
 and my spirit rejoices in God my Savior."
 Luke 1:46–47
She sang of a God who scatters the proud, lifts the humble, fills the hungry, and remembers mercy. Her voice turned the ordinary air holy.
Two women, one older, one young, stood wrapped in divine joy, and heaven leaned close.
 Their laughter became a kind of prophecy, their song a defiance against fear.
 Joy became atmosphere—hope flooding their home and echoing through generations.

DAY 5: JOY: SETTING THE ATMOSPHERE

Reflection:

Joy is not the absence of hardship; it is the quiet confidence that God is near and good in every season. A joyful wife sets the tone of her home; her laughter becomes light, her peace becomes shelter (Phil 4:4; Prov 17:22). True joy is rooted not in circumstances, but in presence—the nearness of a faithful God.

Challenge:

Begin a "Grace List" at dinner this week. Each evening, invite every heart at your table to name one gift from God that day; something seen, felt, or remembered. Let gratitude tune your home to heaven's joy.

Deeper Study:

John 15:11 – Joy made full in Christ
    Romans 12:12 – Rejoice in hope
        Psalm 16:11 – Fullness of joy in God's presence

Prayer

"LORD, restore to me the joy of Your salvation. Let my spirit rejoice in You until my home sings with peace. May my laughter be light that reminds others of Your love."

Which habit or thought pattern most drains joy in our home?
What simple swap—gratitude for complaint, praise for worry, could restore it?

Day 5: Joy: Setting the Atmosphere

A Biblical Woman

DAY 6

Sarah

Respect: Strength Under Order

The desert wind whispered through the tent flaps near Mamre, carrying the scent of dust and bread. Sarah's life had been one long pilgrimage, leaving her homeland, walking beside Abraham through wilderness and wonder, trusting a promise she could not yet see. She had questioned, she had laughed, she had wept. Yet through it all, she stayed, steadfast in spirit, honoring her husband's call while anchoring her heart in God's faithfulness.
Peter later remembered her as a woman of reverence:
"As Sarah obeyed Abraham, calling him lord…"
  1 Peter 3:6
Her respect did not silence her. She spoke with clarity, even courage—urging Abraham to act when hard choices came. But her tone carried honor, her heart aligned under God's design. She trusted the Lord's order more than her own control, and in that trust, she found peace.
In the quiet kneading of flour, in the echo of laughter that filled her tent when Isaac was born, in the long years of waiting and wandering—Sarah's respect became the unseen strength of her home.
True respect is not weakness; it is willful dignity, a heart strong enough to yield because it rests secure in God.

DAY 6: RESPECT: STRENGTH UNDER ORDER

Reflection:

Respect is faith in God's design, strength choosing to honor His order (Eph 5:33; 1 Pet 3:1–4). It is not silence or shrinking, but steady confidence that love flourishes under reverence. Respect builds trust, unites hearts, and anchors peace within a home.

Challenge:

Practice "three acts of respect" today. Name a strength you admire in your husband and speak it out loud. Ask, rather than direct, on one decision. Pray for his calling, that he would walk in courage and wisdom.
Let these small seeds of honor grow into deep-rooted unity.

Deeper Study:

Ephesians 5:33 – Respect your husband
    1 Peter 3:1–4 – A gentle and quiet spirit, precious in God's sight
        Proverbs 14:1 – A wise woman builds her house

Prayer

"LORD, teach me reverence that builds, not silence that shrinks. Give me a spirit both strong and gentle, able to honor, to trust, and to follow You with peace. Let my respect become the melody that steadies my home."

Where am I grasping for control in a place God is asking me to entrust? What might happen if I replaced striving with quiet strength and prayer?

DAY 6: RESPECT: STRENGTH UNDER ORDER

A BIBLICAL WOMAN

DAY 7

Prayerfulness: Covering the House

The tabernacle was thick with the scent of smoke and sacrifice.
 Hannah entered quietly, her shoulders trembling with the weight of years.
 Barrenness had pressed hard on her soul, yet even in grief she turned not away, but toward God.
Kneeling low, lips quivering, she whispered her vow:
"O Lord of hosts, if You will look on Your servant and give me a son,
 I will give him to the Lord all his days."
 1 Samuel 1:11
Eli watched and misunderstood, mistaking her anguish for drunkenness.
 But Hannah, steady and dignified, replied:
"I have been pouring out my soul before the Lord."
 1 Samuel 1:15
Heaven heard.
 In time, Samuel was born, a child of promise, and when her arms had known his weight, she kept her vow and returned him to God.
Her lips overflowed with praise:
"My heart exults in the Lord; my strength is exalted in my God."
 1 Samuel 2:1
Hannah's story reminds us that prayer is not polite formality;
 it is the covering of a home, the shaping of generations,
 and the language through which mothers partner with heaven.

DAY 7: PRAYERFULNESS: COVERING THE HOUSE

Reflection:

Prayer is the roofbeam of a godly home. It holds the household together, unseen yet unshakable. A wife's prayers bless rooms, guard children, and strengthen her husband (Phil 4:6–7; 1 Thess 5:17). Through prayer, she becomes the quiet keeper of peace and the steady heart of her household.

Challenge:

Walk through your home in prayer. Speak blessing over each room—peace in the living room, rest in the bedrooms, joy in the kitchen. End with a prayer over your husband, entrusting his heart and calling to the Lord.

Deeper Study:

Philippians 4:6–7 – Pray about everything
    1 Samuel 1:10–20 – Hannah's prayer answered
        Ephesians 6:18 – Pray in the Spirit on all occasions

Prayer

"LORD, make our house a dwelling of Your presence. Let every wall echo with peace, every room reflect Your goodness, and every heart rest under Your covering. Teach me to be a woman whose prayers build what hands alone cannot."

*What changed within me as I prayed through each room?
Did I sense peace, conviction, gratitude, or renewal?*

Day 7: Prayerfulness: Covering the House

A Biblical Woman

DAY 8

Faithfulness: Marked by Covenant

The streets of Jericho pulsed with fear.
 The city's walls towered high, but the hearts within them trembled.
Amid idols and corruption lived Rahab, a harlot by trade, but her heart had begun to turn toward the whispers of a living God. When two Israelite spies sought refuge, she hid them beneath stalks of flax on her rooftop.
A pounding came at her door, soldiers demanding answers.
 Her voice, steady and sure, did not betray them.
 "Yes, the men came, but I did not know where they went."
As footsteps faded down a false trail, she turned back to the hidden strangers, faith flickering like the oil lamp beside them.
"I know that the Lord has given you the land...
 for the Lord your God, He is God in the heavens above and on the earth beneath."
 Joshua 2:9, 11
Then, with trembling hands, Rahab tied a scarlet cord in her window, a sign of covenant, a mark of faith in the unseen.
When Jericho's walls thundered to the ground, her home stood untouched.
 Faithfulness had drawn a line of mercy across her doorway.
Rahab's scarlet thread still speaks:
 Faithfulness saves families.
 Even in ruin, covenant love stands unbroken.

Day 8: Faithfulness: Marked by Covenant

Reflection:

Faithfulness may feel costly, but it is covenant loyalty, devotion to God above all else. Like Rahab, your steadfast trust can preserve generations and draw mercy over your household. Even when surrounded by fear or uncertainty, faithfulness marks your home with the color of redemption.

Challenge:

Reflect on Hebrews 10:23: "Let us hold fast the confession of our hope without wavering, for He who promised is faithful." Write one "scarlet cord" prayer of faith over your family this week, a promise you will cling to when the walls around you shake.

Deeper Study:

Joshua 2:8–11 – Covenant faith
Hebrews 11:31 – Faith rewarded
James 2:25 – Faith in action

Prayer

"LORD, bind my home with cords of faithfulness that cannot be broken. Teach me to trust You when the world trembles, and to cling to Your promises with unwavering heart. May my devotion draw mercy over generations yet to come."

Where has my faithfulness marked my household like Rahab's cord?
How have I seen God's mercy thread through the story of our home?

Day 8: Faithfulness: Marked by Covenant

A Biblical Woman

DAY 9

Wisdom: Oil for the Lamp

The night deepened, stars flickering over the quiet hills, as ten young women lifted their lamps and waited for the bridegroom.
 Laughter had once filled the air, but as the hours passed, the glow dimmed and eyelids grew heavy.
At midnight, a cry pierced the silence:
"Here is the bridegroom! Come out to meet him!"
   Matthew 25:6
Sudden movement. Scrambling hands. Five lamps flared with readiness, steady, golden light fed by oil kept in secret store. But five others faltered, their flames sputtering into smoke.
"Give us some of your oil," they pleaded.
 But the wise, grieved yet steadfast, answered:
"There will not be enough for us and for you; go rather to the dealers and buy for yourselves."
And while they went, the bridegroom came.
 The wise entered the wedding feast, their lamps bright with devotion. The foolish returned too late, shut outside the door.
Wisdom had not come in a rush of panic, but through quiet preparation.
 It was foresight, discipline, and love that kept the flame alive.
 For the wise, readiness was not duty, it was devotion.

DAY 9: WISDOM: OIL FOR THE LAMP

Reflection:

Wisdom prepares in advance. It is the oil in the lamp, discernment in speech, and readiness in heart. A wise wife guards her home by storing truth and light, keeping faith burning steady even when the night feels long.

Challenge:

Reflect on Proverbs 6:23: "For the commandment is a lamp and the teaching a light." Choose one "lamp verse" this week and place it where your eyes often fall, on the mirror, the fridge, the doorframe.
 Let it remind you daily to keep your oil ready.

Deeper Study:

Matthew 25:1–13 – Watchful wisdom
 Proverbs 9:10 – The fear of the Lord is the beginning of wisdom
 Colossians 4:5 – Walk in wisdom toward outsiders

Prayer

"LORD, fill my lamp with wisdom and keep me ready for You. Teach me to treasure Your truth, to listen with discernment, and to walk in light until You call me home."

Am I storing the oil of wisdom, time in prayer, time in the Word, time listening for His voice? Would I be ready if the Bridegroom came tonight

DAY 9: WISDOM: OIL FOR THE LAMP

A Biblical Woman

DAY 10

The Widow

Sacrifice: Little Becomes Much

The drought had baked the earth hard, each streambed cracked and silent beneath the sun. In the town of Zarephath, a widow bent low beside her fire, gathering a few dry sticks for what she believed would be her final meal. Only a handful of flour and a trickle of oil remained, barely enough for one small cake to share with her son before surrendering to hunger.

Then a stranger appeared, his voice calm yet commanding:

"Bring me a little water in a vessel... and a morsel of bread in your hand."

Her heart ached at the request. She answered with weary honesty:

"I have nothing baked, only a handful of flour in a jar and a little oil in a jug. I am gathering sticks so that we may eat it and die."

1 Kings 17:12

Elijah met her eyes and spoke a promise:

"Do not fear... for the jar of flour shall not be spent, and the jug of oil shall not be empty, until the day the Lord sends rain upon the earth."

With trembling hands, she chose to believe. She gave from her lack—and found herself living in God's abundance.

Day after day, the jar never emptied, and the oil never ran dry.

What she offered in faith became the vessel for her family's miracle.

Little, when placed in God's hands, becomes much.

Reflection:

Servant-heartedness is obedience even in scarcity, offering the little we have and trusting God to make it much. The widow's hands were nearly empty, yet her heart was full of faith. When we surrender our smallness to His greatness, ordinary service becomes the soil of miracles.

Challenge:

Reflect on Galatians 5:13: "Through love, serve one another." Choose one humble task this week, packing a meal, praying for someone, writing a note of encouragement, and do it as quiet worship. Let love turn small things into sacred ones.

Deeper Study:

1 Kings 17:8–16 – God provides through faith
    Luke 21:1–4 – She gave all she had
        Romans 12:1 – Present your bodies as a living sacrifice

Prayer

"LORD, take my ordinary service and multiply it into blessing. When my hands feel empty, remind me that You are my supply. Make my daily acts of love the vessel for Your miracles."

Where might God be asking me to give what feels like my last jar of oil? How might obedience open a door for His provision?

DAY 10: SACRIFICE: LITTLE BECOMES MUCH

A Biblical Woman

DAY 11

Esther

Sacrifice: Little Becomes Much

The marble courts of Persia glittered with gold, yet Esther's heart beat like a drum within her chest.
 The law was unyielding: no one entered the king's presence uninvited and lived.
 But the fate of her people rested on her obedience to a higher call.
She clothed herself in royal robes, spine straight though her knees trembled, and stepped into the throne room.
 Every echo of her footfall carried both fear and faith.
The king's gaze found her.
 Silence hung heavy, the air thick with unseen war.
 Then the golden scepter extended, and mercy triumphed over law.
"What is it, Queen Esther? What is your request?"
Her courage opened the door to deliverance for an entire nation.
Strength did not roar that day, it walked in quietly, clothed in humility and resolve.
 It was the strength of a woman who knew her life was not her own, and that covenant love was worth the risk.
Esther reminds us: true sacrifice often begins with a trembling step, and ends with salvation's victory.

Reflection:

Strength is often quiet, but never passive. It is clothed in dignity, rooted in God's calling, and willing to risk for the sake of others.
True courage does not wait for perfect safety, it steps forward in faith, trusting that obedience opens the way for God's deliverance.

Challenge:

Reflect on Joshua 1:9: "Be strong and courageous. Do not be afraid; for the Lord your God is with you wherever you go." Write down one risk God is asking you to take within your home or calling. Pray over it, then take the first step this week, small or large, but certain.

Deeper Study:

Esther 4:14 – For such a time as this
Psalm 27:1 – The Lord is my light and my salvation; whom shall I fear?
2 Timothy 1:7 – God has given us a spirit of power, love, and self-control

Prayer

"Lord, clothe me with strength for the risks of today. Steady my heart where fear would tremble, and fill me with the quiet courage of Esther. Let my obedience become the doorway for Your deliverance."

Where do I need courage to stand like Esther, "for such a time as this"? What fear must bow to faith before I can move forward?

DAY 11: SACRIFICE: LITTLE BECOMES MUCH

A Biblical Woman

DAY 12

Sarah

Joy: Laughter of Promise

The tent flaps swayed gently in the desert breeze as Sarah cradled her son, her aged arms trembling with both wonder and delight.

For decades she had carried the ache of barrenness, the long silence of waiting, the weight of a promise that seemed forgotten.

And then, at last, laughter filled her tent.

She named him Isaac, meaning "laughter," for God had turned her sorrow into song.

"God has made laughter for me," she said,

"and everyone who hears will laugh over me."

Genesis 21:6

Her laughter was no longer disbelief—it was deliverance.

No longer bitter, it was beautiful.

It rose like morning light, a testimony to the God who fulfills every word He speaks.

Sarah's joy rippled through generations.

Her laughter became a legacy, a reminder that the promises of God never expire, no matter how long the waiting or how barren the season.

For the woman who trusts His timing, joy always comes in due season.

DAY 12: JOY: LAUGHTER OF PROMISE

Reflection:

Joy is a witness. When God turns mourning into laughter, our homes become sanctuaries of hope, places where His promises echo through every room. Sarah's laughter reminds us that joy is not fleeting emotion, but living testimony that God keeps His word.

Challenge:

Reflect on Philippians 4:4: "Rejoice in the Lord always; again I will say, rejoice." Share one moment of joy with your family today, tell a story of God's faithfulness, laugh freely, or sing praise together. Let your home ring with the sound of rejoicing.

Deeper Study:

Genesis 21:1–7 – Promised joy
  Habakkuk 3:17–19 – Rejoice anyway
    Psalm 16:11 – Fullness of joy in God's presence

Prayer

"LORD, let joy rise in me like Sarah's laughter—pure, unexpected, and rooted in Your promises. May my rejoicing become a light that fills my home and strengthens the faith of generations to come."

*Where has God turned my disbelief into joy, as He did for Sarah?
What long wait has now become a testimony of His faithfulness?*

DAY 12: JOY: LAUGHTER OF PROMISE

A Biblical Woman

DAY 13
Rebekah

Respect: Honor Builds Home

Across the wide, sunlit field, Rebekah saw the camels drawing near.
 Dust rose in the distance as her heart quickened, there, walking toward her, was Isaac.
Without hesitation, she dismounted and drew a veil over her face, a simple act of honor, yet one filled with meaning.
 It spoke of reverence, readiness, and quiet confidence in God's design.
Isaac took her into his mother Sarah's tent, and she became his wife.
"And he loved her."
 Genesis 24:67
Her veil was more than fabric; it was faith in motion, an outward sign of inward respect.
 In that gesture, Rebekah showed what every wise woman knows:
 Honor invites love, and respect builds the peace a home needs to thrive.

Reflection:

Respect is strength under order. It builds trust and steadies the heart of a marriage, rooting it in reverence for God's design. When a wife honors her husband, she invites peace, unity, and blessing into her home.

Challenge:

Reflect on Ephesians 5:33: "Let the wife see that she respects her husband." Speak one word of admiration over your husband today, something that affirms his calling, steadies his spirit, or reminds him of who God made him to be.

Deeper Study:

Genesis 24:15–20 – Generous respect
    Romans 12:10 – Honor one another above yourselves
    Philippians 2:3 – In humility, value others above yourself

Prayer

"LORD, help me to honor my husband in ways that honor You. Teach me that reverence is not weakness, but wisdom, an act of worship that builds peace within my home."

How can I, like Rebekah, show honor through humble service? What simple gesture might speak reverence more powerfully than words?

DAY 13: RESPECT: HONOR BUILDS HOME

A BIBLICAL WOMAN

DAY 14

Anna

Prayerfulness: Persistent Prayer

The temple stones were cool beneath her feet, their edges worn smooth by years of worship.

Morning light spilled through the courts, glinting across the bronze altar as incense curled toward heaven. Among the worshipers moved an elderly woman, her step slow but her spirit alight with expectancy.

Her name was Anna—a prophetess of the tribe of Asher.

Widowed after only seven years of marriage, she had given the rest of her life to one pursuit: the presence of God.

Day after day, she lingered in the temple, fasting, praying, and keeping vigil for the Redeemer promised to Israel.

While the years rolled on and kingdoms changed, Anna remained.

Her prayers became the rhythm of her days, her life an unbroken offering before the Lord. Then, one morning, the promise walked in.

Mary and Joseph entered the temple, carrying the infant Jesus in their arms.

As Anna looked upon the Child, her weary eyes filled with holy recognition.

"And coming up at that very hour she began to give thanks to God
and to speak of Him to all who were waiting for the redemption of Jerusalem."
    Luke 2:38

Joy welled up like a spring that could no longer be contained.

Her decades of devotion found their answer in the face of a baby.

She gave thanks and became the first to proclaim the Redeemer to those still waiting in hope.

Anna's faith was not marked by comfort or applause, but by perseverance.

She teaches us that prayer is not simply something we do, it's who we become when we dwell with God long enough.

And when the promise finally appears, those who have been praying are the first to recognize His presence.

Reflection:

Prayer is never wasted; it is seed sown into God's eternal purposes.
   Like Anna, we are called to persistence and expectancy, believing that unseen prayers still move heaven. In quiet faith, every whispered petition becomes part of His unfolding redemption.

Challenge:

Set aside ten quiet minutes today for prayerful stillness. Silence distractions, steady your heart, and listen for the gentle whisper of God's Spirit. Let stillness become the space where faith takes root.

Deeper Study:

Luke 2:36–38 – Devoted prayer
   1 Thessalonians 5:17 – Pray continually
      Colossians 4:2 – Continue steadfastly in prayer

Prayer

"LORD, *make me steadfast like Anna. Teach me to wait well, eyes open to recognize Your presence, lips ready to proclaim Your redemption.*
   Let my prayers outlast my seasons, bearing fruit in Your perfect time."

Where is God inviting me to persevere in prayer, even when the answer feels long delayed? What promise might He be preparing to fulfill in His perfect time?

DAY 14: PRAYERFULNESS: PERSISTENT PRAYER

A Biblical Woman

DAY 15

Faithfulness: Enduring Loyalty

The road from Moab to Judah stretched long and uncertain. Naomi's heart was scarred by loss—her husband and sons gone, her hands empty, her hope dim. "Do not call me Naomi," she said. "Call me Mara, for the Almighty has dealt very bitterly with me." (Ruth 1:20)
Yet even in sorrow, her quiet faith spoke louder than her pain.
 Her devotion, though weary, still pointed toward the God she trusted.
 And beside her, Ruth saw it.
When Naomi urged her to turn back, Ruth clung to her with unwavering love:
"Where you go I will go, and where you stay I will stay.
 Your people shall be my people, and your God my God."
 Ruth 1:16
Naomi's steadfast faith became the seed of redemption.
 Through her guidance, Ruth found Boaz—and from their union came the lineage of David, and ultimately, of Christ.
Faithfulness does not always look triumphant; sometimes it simply keeps walking.
 Naomi's loyalty in suffering became the soil where God planted legacy.

DAY 15: FAITHFULNESS: ENDURING LOYALTY

Reflection:

Even in grief, Naomi's steadfastness spoke louder than words.
Faithfulness is not perfection, it is endurance rooted in God's covenant. When we keep walking toward Him, even with weary hearts, our steady trust can become the very witness that shapes generations.

Challenge:

Write a prayer of blessing for your children or spiritual daughters, entrusting their future to God's faithful hands. Pray that they will see His goodness in every season, and carry forward the legacy of your faith.

Deeper Study:

Ruth 1:16–17 – Covenant loyalty
Psalm 119:90 – Faith endures through all generations
2 Timothy 1:5 – Generational faith

Prayer

"LORD, let my faithfulness, even in hardship, draw others closer to You.
When I cannot see the fruit of endurance, remind me that You are still at work,
turning sorrow to seed and legacy to life."

*Where has my quiet faith influenced others without me realizing it?
Whose story might God be writing through my perseverance?*

Day 15: Faithfulness: Enduring Loyalty

A BIBLICAL WOMAN

DAY 16
Huldah

Wisdom: Fearless Truth

The air in Jerusalem was tense with awakening.
 The long-lost Book of the Law had been found in the temple, and when its words were read aloud, King Josiah tore his robes in grief. The people trembled. Who could tell them what it meant?
They sought not a priest or a prophet, but a woman, Huldah, the prophetess who dwelt in Jerusalem.
When the king's messengers came, she did not shrink before their authority.
 She stood firm and spoke the word of the Lord with clarity and courage:
"Thus says the Lord, I am bringing disaster upon this place… but because your heart was penitent and you humbled yourself before the Lord, you shall be gathered to your grave in peace."
  2 Kings 22:16, 19–20
Huldah's wisdom was not shaped by opinion or fear of men, it was revelation rooted in reverence for God.
 In a time of compromise, she became a voice of truth, guiding a king and a nation back to repentance.
Her story reminds us that wisdom is fearless when it flows from faithfulness.
 To speak truth in love, even when few listen, is one of the highest acts of courage.

DAY 16: WISDOM: FEARLESS TRUTH

Reflection:

True wisdom is bold, uncompromising, and anchored in the Word of God. It listens before it speaks, discerns before it decides, and stands firm even when truth is costly. Like Huldah, we are called to be steady voices of clarity in a confused world.

Challenge:

Before making a decision this week, pause and seek God's wisdom in prayer. Ask Him to reveal His will through His Word, and write down what He shows you. Let discernment be the first step, not the last resort.

Deeper Study:

James 1:5 – Ask God for wisdom
   Proverbs 2:6 – The Lord gives wisdom
      Colossians 3:16 – Let the Word of Christ dwell richly in you

Prayer

*"Lord, grant me wisdom to discern and courage to declare Your truth.
Let my words be guided by Your Spirit—firm, faithful, and full of grace.
Make me fearless in love and unwavering in obedience."*

Where do I need to speak God's wisdom with courage?
What fear or hesitation must I surrender to walk boldly in truth?

DAY 16: WISDOM: FEARLESS TRUTH

A BIBLICAL WOMAN

DAY 17

Sacrifice: Hidden Courage

Panic echoed through the palace halls as Athaliah seized the throne, determined to destroy every descendant of David. The royal family of Judah was cut down, and the covenant line seemed moments from extinction.
But in the midst of that chaos, one woman acted with quiet resolve.
Jehosheba, daughter of King Jehoram and sister to Ahaziah, gathered the infant prince Joash into her arms and fled.
Through dark corridors she carried him to safety, hiding him within the temple of the Lord.
For six long years, while Athaliah ruled with violence and fear, Jehosheba kept silent vigil.
Her courage was unseen, her devotion steady, her trust fixed on God's promise.
"But Jehosheba... took Joash the son of Ahaziah and stole him away... and hid him in the house of the Lord six years."
2 Kings 11:2–3
Her hidden obedience preserved the covenant that David's line would endure.
Because one faithful woman chose courage in secret, a kingdom was restored and the word of God fulfilled.
Jehosheba reminds us that some of the greatest acts of faith happen in quiet places—where loyalty costs much, but legacy is born.

DAY 17: SACRIFICE: HIDDEN COURAGE

Reflection:

Sacrifice often looks like unseen courage, faithful obedience that protects God's promises for generations yet to come. Jehosheba's bravery was hidden from the world, but heaven recorded every act. True sacrifice trusts that what is done in secret can shape the future in ways only God can see.

Challenge:

Identify one area where you can make a hidden sacrifice this week, something unseen but deeply impactful. Offer it to the Lord without announcement or reward, trusting that quiet obedience builds eternal legacy.

Deeper Study:

Romans 12:1 – Living sacrifice
    John 15:13 – Lay down one's life for others
        Philippians 2:4 – Look to the interests of others

Prayer

"LORD, help me lay down my comfort so that Your promises are preserved in my family. Teach me to value the hidden work, to guard what is sacred, and to trust that quiet faithfulness changes the generations to come."

What future blessing might depend on my sacrifice today?
How might God be inviting me to guard His promises in my own home?

DAY 17: SACRIFICE: HIDDEN COURAGE

A BIBLICAL WOMAN

DAY 18

Jael

Strength: Decisive Action

The clash of battle thundered in the distance as Sisera, commander of Canaan's army, fled for his life.

Exhausted and desperate for refuge, he came upon the tent of Jael, the wife of Heber the Kenite.

She stepped forward with calm hospitality, offering milk and a blanket, her demeanor gentle but her spirit resolute.

When Sisera fell into a deep sleep, Jael reached for the tools of her ordinary life—a hammer and a tent peg.

With unwavering hand, she acted, and through her obedience, the Lord delivered Israel from its oppressor.

"So God subdued Jabin the king of Canaan before the people of Israel."
— Judges 4:23

Jael's strength was not born of rage or recklessness, but of discernment and courage.

While armies clashed in the open field, God worked deliverance through one woman's decisive faith behind closed walls.

True strength listens for God's timing, then acts without hesitation.

It is courage guided by conviction, not impulse—a readiness to do what is right, even when the task is hard.

DAY 18: STRENGTH: DECISIVE ACTION

Reflection:

Strength is not only found in muscle or might—it is the courage to act when God calls. True strength listens first, then moves in faith, trusting that His power will steady each step.

Challenge:

Face one fear this week with courage, trusting that God's strength goes before you. Let obedience, not comfort, determine your next move.

Deeper Study:

Nehemiah 8:10 – The joy of the Lord is your strength
Psalm 18:32 – God arms me with strength
2 Corinthians 12:9 – His power is made perfect in weakness

Prayer

"LORD, fill me with boldness and strength to act when You call me to move. Quiet my fear, steady my resolve, and let courage rise in me until Your will is done."

Where is God calling me to act with courage, even when it feels uncomfortable? What would obedience look like if I trusted His strength more than my own?

Day 18: Strength: Decisive Action

A Biblical Woman

DAY 19

Miriam

Joy: Victorious Praise

The waves crashed shut behind them, swallowing Pharaoh's chariots beneath the sea.
 Israel stood on the far shore, the salt air thick with awe and relief.
 For the first time in generations, they were free.
Then Miriam, the prophetess and sister of Moses, lifted a tambourine in her hand.
 Rhythm met redemption as she led the women forward in song and dance, joy spilling from her soul like sunlight after storm.
"Sing to the Lord, for He has triumphed gloriously;
 the horse and rider He has thrown into the sea."
 Exodus 15:21
Her joy was not quiet, it was contagious, a declaration that God's victory deserved celebration.
 What began as trembling on the seashore became worship in motion.
Miriam's song reminds us that praise is not merely response—it is warfare.
 Joy is how the faithful remember that the same God who parts seas still triumphs today.

DAY 19: JOY: VICTORIOUS PRAISE

Reflection:

Joy multiplies when we share it. Praise turns deliverance into testimony and gratitude into strength. When we lift our voices like Miriam, our homes become sanctuaries of rejoicing, reminding all who hear that God still triumphs gloriously.

Challenge:

Begin or end your day with a song of thanksgiving. Sing it aloud in your home, letting praise rise through your walls and over your worries. Joy grows when it's expressed.

Deeper Study:

Psalm 30:11 – Mourning turned to dancing
Philippians 4:4 – Rejoice in the Lord always
Habakkuk 3:18 – Yet I will rejoice in the Lord

Prayer

"LORD, turn my gratitude into bold joy that others can see and join. Teach me to celebrate Your faithfulness with a fearless heart and a song that gives You glory."

Where has God given me victory, and how can I rejoice boldly?
What song of praise could I raise to mark His faithfulness today?

DAY 19: JOY: VICTORIOUS PRAISE

A Biblical Woman

DAY 20

Respect: Honorable Service

Far from the crowded streets of Corinth, Phoebe served faithfully in the seaside town of Cenchreae.

Her work was steady, her devotion unshaken. She was known among believers not for loudness or position, but for her faithfulness in the small and sacred tasks that sustained the church.

When Paul prepared to send his letter to the Romans, a message that would shape the faith of generations, he entrusted it to her care.

"I commend to you our sister Phoebe, a deacon of the church at Cenchreae,
 that you may receive her in the Lord in a manner worthy of the saints
 and assist her in whatever she may need from you,
 for she has been a benefactor of many and of myself as well."
 Romans 16:1–2

Phoebe carried more than parchment that day, she carried the weight of trust, the message of the gospel, and the honor of her calling.

Her service was humble yet vital, proving that respect is not a title but a posture of the heart.

Through grace, diligence, and faithfulness, she showed that honorable service is itself an act of worship.

DAY 20: RESPECT: HONORABLE SERVICE

Reflection:

Respect is shown through action, through faithful service, responsibility, and honor toward God's people. True respect doesn't seek recognition; it expresses love by carrying out each task with diligence and grace. Like Phoebe, we honor God best when our service is steady, humble, and worthy of trust.

Challenge:

Find one practical way to serve your household or church with dignity today, no matter how small. Do it quietly, as worship, knowing that every act done in love honors the Lord.

Deeper Study:

Romans 16:1–2 – Worthy of honor
Philippians 2:3 – In humility, value others above yourself
1 Peter 2:17 – Show proper respect to everyone

Prayer

"LORD, may my service be honorable before You and respected by those who see Your work in me. Teach me to serve with quiet strength and faithful hands, so that my life becomes a reflection of Your grace."

How can I, like Phoebe, model respect through honorable service? What opportunities has God placed before me to serve faithfully and with grace?

DAY 20: RESPECT: HONORABLE SERVICE

A BIBLICAL WOMAN

DAY 21

Mary

Prayerfulness: Prayerful Surrender

Mary's voice rose in prayer, her heart overflowing with praise.
After hearing Elizabeth's blessing, she could no longer contain her gratitude.
"My soul magnifies the Lord,
and my spirit rejoices in God my Savior."
Luke 1:46–47
Her words, what we now call the Magnificat, were more than song.
They were a prayer of surrender, a declaration that God's mercy reaches the lowly and His promises never fail.
Mary rejoiced not in her own strength, but in the power of the Almighty to lift the humble and bring His salvation near.
This was no timid whisper. It was a bold, prophetic cry of trust, a young woman yielding fully to the will of God.
Through her prayer, Mary became a vessel for divine redemption, her voice joining heaven's chorus.
Her song still echoes through the centuries as an anthem of surrender, teaching us that prayer is not simply asking, it is yielding, praising, and believing that God's promises are already true.

DAY 21: PRAYERFULNESS: PRAYERFUL SURRENDER

Reflection:

Prayer is most powerful when it magnifies God above all else.
Like Mary, we learn that true surrender is not silent resignation but joyful trust, lifting our eyes from ourselves to the greatness of our Savior. When our prayers glorify Him first, they align heaven's power with earth's need.

Challenge:

Pray Mary's Magnificat aloud today (Luke 1:46–55). Let her words become your own song of surrender and praise, a declaration that God is mighty, merciful, and faithful through every generation.

Deeper Study:

Luke 1:46–55 – Mary's song of surrender
Philippians 4:6 – Prayer and petition with thanksgiving
1 Thessalonians 5:16–18 – Rejoice and pray continually

Prayer

"Lord, let my soul magnify You. Teach me to pray with bold surrender and joyful trust, as Mary did. May my words and my worship reflect Your greatness and draw others to Your presence."

How can my prayers magnify God rather than myself? What happens when gratitude, not worry, becomes the starting point of my prayer?

Day 21: Prayerfulness: Prayerful Surrender

A BIBLICAL WOMAN

DAY 22

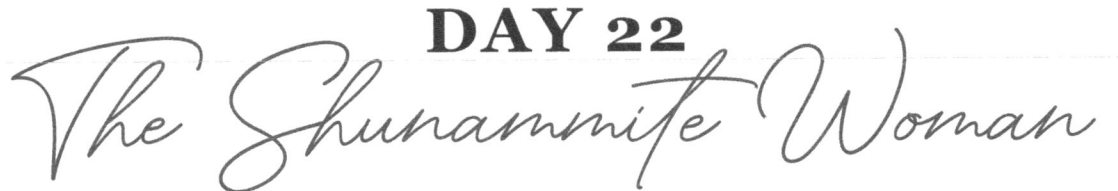

Faithfulness: Unshaken Trust

In the hills of Shunem lived a woman known for grace and hospitality. Whenever the prophet Elisha passed by, she welcomed him to rest and built a small upper room for him, a quiet space of care and faith. Her kindness was simple, steady, and sincere.

She asked for nothing in return, but God noticed her faithfulness. Through Elisha, He promised her a son, a miracle for a woman long barren. Joy filled her home, laughter echoing through the very halls that had once been silent.

Years later, that laughter was silenced. Her son fell ill in the fields and died in her arms. The promise seemed broken, but her spirit did not shatter. Without delay, she laid the boy on the prophet's bed, saddled her donkey, and prepared to find Elisha.

Her husband asked why she would go that day, and she answered with steady faith, "It is well." 2 Kings 4:23

Those words were not denial—they were declaration. Even in heartbreak, she believed the God who gives life could also restore it.

When she reached Elisha, her cry was raw and reverent: "Did I ask for a son, my lord? Did I not say, 'Do not deceive me?'" (v. 28) Her faith was fierce, not fragile—unwilling to surrender hope until God moved.

Elisha came to her home, prayed, and the child's breath returned. Her faithfulness became a living testimony that what we place in God's hands, even in death or disappointment, can live again by His power.

DAY 22: FAITHFULNESS: UNSHAKEN TRUST

Reflection:

Faithfulness clings to God's promises even when circumstances seem hopeless. Like the Shunammite woman, we are called to anchor our trust not in what we see, but in who He is. Faith endures the waiting and declares God's goodness before the breakthrough comes.

Challenge:

In one area of fear or uncertainty this week, speak the words, "It is well." Let your declaration become an act of worship—a statement of trust that God is still at work.

Deeper Study:

2 Kings 4:18–37 – Faith rewarded
    Hebrews 11:35 – Women of faith
    Psalm 112:7 – Heart steadfast, trusting in the Lord

Prayer

"Lord, give me unshaken trust in You when storms arise. Teach me to declare 'It is well' even before the miracle comes. Let my faith become a shelter for those around me and a testimony of Your power to restore."

How does my faith steady my household? What might change if my first response to trouble was confidence in God's faithfulness?

DAY 22: FAITHFULNESS: UNSHAKEN TRUST

A BIBLICAL WOMAN

DAY 23

Priscilla

Wisdom: Guided Truth

The marketplace of Ephesus hummed with the clatter of sandals and the scent of spices. In a modest home tucked between whitewashed walls, Priscilla leaned over a table of open scrolls. The lamp's flame flickered on her face as she reread the words of the prophets, truth she and her husband, Aquila, had carried like treasure since leaving Rome.

Word spread of a man named Apollos, an eloquent preacher from Alexandria. His voice filled the synagogue, passionate, persuasive, but incomplete. He spoke of repentance and John's baptism, yet his understanding of Jesus was not yet full. Priscilla and Aquila listened quietly, exchanging a glance that said everything: He has zeal, but not yet light. Afterwards, they approached him gently. There was no pride in Priscilla's tone, no correction in her posture, only warmth. "Apollos," she said, "you speak beautifully of God's promises. Come, dine with us, and hear how they've been fulfilled." That night, in the glow of the lamp, she unrolled the scroll and spoke of the risen Christ.

"The word of Christ dwell in you richly, teaching and admonishing one another in all wisdom."

Colossians 3:16

By morning, Apollos's message burned with new fire. He would go on to strengthen the churches and preach Christ with boldness.

"A word fitly spoken is like apples of gold in settings of silver."

Proverbs 25:11

The seed was sown in a quiet home by a woman whose wisdom made room for revelation. Priscilla's life reminds us that divine wisdom doesn't seek a platform, it seeks a person, guiding hearts gently toward the fullness of truth.

DAY 23: WISDOM: GUIDED TRUTH

Reflection:

Wisdom is not only understanding truth but guiding others toward it with grace. True wisdom listens before it speaks and builds before it corrects. Like Priscilla, we are called to teach with humility, inviting others into revelation rather than forcing it upon them.

Challenge:

Share one biblical truth gently with someone who needs encouragement this week. Let your words carry both compassion and conviction, pointing hearts toward Christ.

Deeper Study:

Acts 18:24–26 – Wise instruction
    Proverbs 31:26 – Wisdom speaks with kindness
    Colossians 3:16 – The word of Christ dwells richly

Prayer

"LORD, give me the humility to listen and the courage to speak truth in love. Let my words illuminate, not intimidate—building others up in Your wisdom and grace."

How can I use wisdom to strengthen another's walk with Christ?
Where is God giving me opportunity to speak truth with gentleness?

Day 23: Wisdom: Guided Truth

A BIBLICAL WOMAN

DAY 24

Rizpah

Sacrifice: Unyielding Devotion

The hill was silent except for the whisper of wind through the trees.

Beneath that lonely sky, a mother spread a rough cloak of sackcloth over the bare rock. Rizpah, daughter of Aiah, had come to keep vigil where her two sons had fallen. They had been executed in a political reckoning, a debt paid for King Saul's sin, and left exposed to the elements.

No one came to mourn them. No one, except their mother.

From the beginning of the harvest until the rains returned, Rizpah stayed.

Day after day, she guarded her sons' bodies from scavenging birds.

At night she kept a small fire, driving away the beasts that prowled in the dark. "Many waters cannot quench love, neither can floods drown it."

— Song of Solomon 8:7

Her grief was raw, her body weary, but she would not move. The world might forget, but she would not.

News of her vigil reached King David, and his heart was pierced.

Because of Rizpah's steadfast devotion, he gathered the bones of Saul, Jonathan, and the slain men, giving them an honorable burial in their family tomb.

"Blessed are those who mourn, for they shall be comforted."

— Matthew 5:4

Imagine her beneath the gray sky, hair matted with dust, hands rough from keeping watch, eyes fixed on the horizon.

She could not bring back what was lost, but her sacrifice redeemed their memory. Her presence turned a place of death into a sanctuary of love.

Rizpah teaches us that sacrifice is not always a single act, it can be the long obedience of love that refuses to let go.

She did not lift a sword, yet she fought for dignity.

She did not demand vengeance, yet she moved a king's heart.

Her watch became her worship.

DAY 24: SACRIFICE: UNYIELDING DEVOTION

Reflection:

Sacrifice often means staying in the hard place until God restores honor to what was broken. Like Rizpah, faith sometimes looks like endurance, holding vigil in prayer and trust until heaven moves. Love that refuses to leave becomes the altar where God's justice and mercy meet.

Challenge:

Stand firm in one place of intercession for your family this week. Pray faithfully over what feels forgotten, believing that God sees and will redeem in His time.

Deeper Study:

2 Samuel 21:10 – Steadfast vigil
    Romans 12:12 – Patient in affliction, faithful in prayer
    Galatians 6:9 – Do not grow weary in doing good

Prayer

"LORD, *teach me Rizpah's kind of love—steady, selfless, and strong enough to wait until Your justice comes. When I'm weary, remind me that You see. Let my faithfulness bear witness to Your redeeming power.*"

Where is God asking me to remain devoted, even in hardship?
What might He be restoring as I choose to stay faithful in prayer?

DAY 24: SACRIFICE: UNYIELDING DEVOTION

A BIBLICAL WOMAN

DAY 25

Pharaoh's Daughter

Strength: Courageous Compassion

The Nile shimmered beneath the morning sun as Pharaoh's daughter stepped down from the palace steps to bathe. The air smelled of river reeds and silt, ordinary, peaceful, yet the water hid sorrow. Her father had commanded that every Hebrew son be cast into it, swallowed by the current. But that morning, the stillness broke with a cry, faint but alive. Among the reeds drifted a small basket, sealed with pitch. The princess drew it near, lifted the lid, and looked down into the face of a Hebrew baby. His eyes blinked up at her, helpless and full of life. In that moment, compassion overpowered fear. She knew her father's decree. She knew the risk. And yet she could not turn away.

"When she opened it, she saw the child, and behold, the baby was crying. She took pity on him."

Exodus 2:6

"This must be one of the Hebrew children," she whispered. Then a young girl, Moses' sister, stepped forward and asked, "Shall I go and call you a nurse from the Hebrew women?" The princess nodded, unknowingly returning the child into his mother's care. Pharaoh's daughter did not lift a weapon or command an army. Her courage was quieter, deeper, the strength to protect life when obedience to God required defiance of man.

"Speak up for those who cannot speak for themselves."

Proverbs 31:8

Through one act of fearless mercy, she rescued the deliverer of Israel. Her story reminds us that true strength is not measured in might but in mercy, born when compassion dares to act.

DAY 25: STRENGTH: COURAGEOUS COMPASSION

Reflection:

True strength often takes the form of compassion that dares to defy fear. Like Pharaoh's daughter, we are called to protect life and honor God even when courage comes at a cost. Strength guided by mercy becomes a vessel of redemption.

Challenge:

Defend or protect someone vulnerable this week, whether through words of encouragement, an act of kindness, or a moment of quiet advocacy. Let your compassion speak louder than fear.

Deeper Study:

Exodus 2:5–10 – The rescue of Moses
    Psalm 82:3 – Defend the weak and the fatherless
    Isaiah 1:17 – Seek justice, defend the oppressed

Prayer

"LORD, give me courage to act with compassion even when it costs me. Let my mercy become a shield for those You love, and my strength be known by how I protect the vulnerable in Your name."

Where can I show courageous compassion today? Whom is God placing before me to defend, comfort, or uplift in His name?

DAY 25: STRENGTH: COURAGEOUS COMPASSION

A BIBLICAL WOMAN

DAY 26

Joy: Faithful Rejoicing

In the quiet hills of Judea, a woman named Elizabeth carried a miracle long promised but long delayed.

Her hair was silver, her hands weathered, yet her heart was alive with wonder.

For years she had borne the ache of barrenness, the whispers of pity, the silence of unanswered prayer.

But now, at last, the Lord had remembered her.

Life stirred within her womb, John, the forerunner of Christ, proof that no prayer is forgotten.

One afternoon, her door burst open with the sound of footsteps.

It was Mary, her young cousin, glowing with her own secret: she too carried a child, conceived not by man but by the Spirit of God.

The moment Mary's greeting reached Elizabeth's ears, the baby leapt within her, and she was filled with the Holy Spirit.

"Blessed are you among women, and blessed is the fruit of your womb!"

Luke 1:42

The two women stood in the doorway of history, one old, one young, rejoicing together in the faithfulness of God.

The world outside might not yet understand what was unfolding, but heaven was already singing.

Their laughter mingled with praise; their joy became prophecy.

Elizabeth teaches us that joy is not bound by time but rooted in trust.

Even after years of silence, she rejoiced when she saw God move, and she celebrated the miracle of another as fiercely as her own.

DAY 26: JOY: FAITHFUL REJOICING

Reflection:

Joy grows in hearts that celebrate God's promises—even the ones fulfilled in others first. Like Elizabeth, we are invited to rejoice not only in our own answered prayers but in the blessings that reveal God's faithfulness around us. True joy multiplies when shared.

Challenge:

Joy grows in hearts that celebrate God's promises—even the ones fulfilled in others first. Like Elizabeth, we are invited to rejoice not only in our own answered prayers but in the blessings that reveal God's faithfulness around us. True joy multiplies when shared.

Deeper Study:

Luke 1:39–45 – Elizabeth's joy
    Philippians 4:4 – Rejoice in the Lord always
    Romans 12:15 – Rejoice with those who rejoice

Prayer

"LORD, make my heart like Elizabeth's, ready to rejoice, to bless, and to see Your hand at work in every good thing. Teach me to find joy in Your faithfulness, even before my own prayers are answered."

Where can I choose joy in someone else's blessing today? What would change in my heart if I celebrated every answered prayer, mine or another's—as proof of His goodness?

DAY 26: JOY: FAITHFUL REJOICING

A BIBLICAL WOMAN

DAY 27

Martha

Respect: Reverent Service

The little village of Bethany was alive with the sounds of preparation.

Martha's home bustled as it always did when Jesus came to visit, water jars clinking, bread baking, herbs crushed for the evening meal.

Every detail mattered to her; hospitality was her language of honor.

As others sat at the Teacher's feet, she moved from hearth to table, her hands never still, her heart full yet restless.

Finally, she could hold her tongue no longer. "Lord," she said, her voice breaking with weariness, "do You not care that my sister has left me to serve alone? Tell her to help me."

Jesus turned to her with tenderness, not rebuke.

"Martha, Martha, you are anxious and troubled about many things, but one thing is necessary."

Luke 10:41–42

In that moment, she understood, service is holy, but worship is higher still. Respect for Christ meant not only serving Him, but also listening when He spoke.

Later, when her brother Lazarus died, it was Martha who ran to meet Jesus first.

Her heart had grown steadfast through loss and love alike.

"Lord, I believe that You are the Christ, the Son of God, who is coming into the world."

John 11:27

She no longer needed to prove her devotion; she had learned to rest in it.

Martha's story reminds us that respect is more than labor, it is the balance between doing and being, serving and listening, acting and adoring.

Reflection:

True respect begins with honoring Christ's presence more than our performance. Like Martha, we learn that serving is holy, but sitting at His feet comes first. Our work finds peace when it flows from worship, not worry.

Challenge:

Before serving today, pause and invite Jesus into your work. Ask Him to order your steps and calm your spirit, so that everything you do reflects His peace.

Deeper Study:

Luke 10:38–42 – One thing needed
John 11:21–27 – Faith renewed
Psalm 46:10 – Be still and know that I am God

Prayer

"LORD, *teach me Martha's balance, hands that serve with love, and a heart that honors You first. Quiet my anxious striving and make my work an act of worship in Your presence.*"

Where is God inviting me to trade striving for sacred stillness?
How might my service change if I began every task by listening first?

Day 27: Respect: Reverent Service

A BIBLICAL WOMAN

DAY 28

Lois

Prayerfulness: Generational Faith

In the quiet city of Lystra, a young boy named Timothy grew beneath the steady love of two women, his mother Eunice and his grandmother Lois. Their home was modest, tucked among clay streets where Greek voices mixed with Jewish prayers. The world around them was changing, full of idols and ideas, but inside those walls, faith was still spoken like a familiar song.

Each morning, Lois lit a small lamp before dawn, unrolling the worn scrolls of the Torah. Her voice was soft yet sure as she read aloud the promises of God. Timothy would listen, still rubbing sleep from his eyes, while Eunice explained what it meant that the Messiah would come. In those early lessons, faith took root, not through sermons or spectacle, but through the quiet repetition of truth in the hands of a mother and grandmother.

Years later, when the apostle Paul met Timothy, he recognized something in the young man's eyes, steady conviction, humble courage. "I am reminded," Paul wrote, "of your sincere faith, which first lived in your grandmother Lois and in your mother Eunice, and I am persuaded now lives in you also." Lois never stood before crowds or wrote epistles, but her legacy preached louder than words.

She reminds us that generational faith is not just inherited, it's lived in front of those who watch us most closely. Her life was a living Scripture, written line by line through patience, prayer, and love.

DAY 28: PRAYERFULNESS: GENERATIONAL FAITH

Reflection:

Legacy begins at home. A single faithful life can ripple through generations, shaping hearts we may never meet. Like Lois, we build inheritance not through wealth or recognition, but through the quiet consistency of faith lived daily before those who watch and learn.

Challenge:

Speak one word of faith or blessing to the next generation this week. Encourage a child, grandchild, or spiritual son or daughter with the reminder that God's promises are for them too.

Deeper Study:

2 Timothy 1:5 – Faith passed down
    Psalm 78:4 – Declare His works to the next generation
        Deuteronomy 6:6–7 – Teach them diligently

Prayer

"LORD, let my life echo like Lois's, steadfast, sincere, and full of Your truth. Make my faith a living inheritance, passed from heart to heart, until generations yet unborn know and trust You."

How can I model faith that endures beyond my lifetime? What daily habits of prayer or devotion will sow faith into those who follow?

Day 28: Prayerfulness: Generational Faith

A BIBLICAL WOMAN

DAY 29

Eunice

Faithfulness: Marked by Covenant

The morning sun filtered through the shutters of a small home in Lystra, painting golden lines across a humble table.
 A young mother sat there, her son beside her, both bent over the Scriptures.
 Eunice's voice was calm and steady as she traced the words with her finger, teaching Timothy the promises she had once learned at her mother's knee.
Outside, the streets buzzed with trade and talk of Greek gods and Roman rule.
 But inside their home was a sanctuary of faith—a covenant preserved in prayer.
 Eunice, a Jewish believer married to a Greek husband, lived between two worlds. Her faith did not shout; it shone. In her words, her patience, and her daily devotion, she built an altar no empire could silence.
"From infancy you have known the Holy Scriptures, which are able to make you wise for salvation through faith in Christ Jesus." — 2 Timothy 3:15
Years later, that boy would walk beside the apostle Paul, carrying the gospel into cities and nations.
 But before he ever preached from the scrolls, he first heard Scripture spoken in his mother's voice. Her teaching became his compass; her prayers, his protection; her faith, his foundation.
Eunice teaches us that faithfulness begins in the ordinary moments—at the breakfast table, beside the lamp, in the daily rhythm of love and correction.
 Every word sown into a child's heart becomes seed for the kingdom, marked by covenant and nourished by grace.

Reflection:

The greatest sermons are often whispered between generations. Faith is most powerfully taught not from pulpits, but from tables, car rides, and bedtime prayers. Like Eunice, we shape eternity when we teach God's truth in the ordinary moments of love and life.

Challenge:

Teach one verse, one truth, or one story of God's faithfulness to someone younger this week. Let the Word you share become a seed planted for the future.

Deeper Study:

2 Timothy 3:14–15 – From infancy, known the Scriptures
    Deuteronomy 11:18–19 – Teach your children diligently
    Proverbs 22:6 – Train up a child in the way he should go

Prayer

"LORD, give me Eunice's heart—to teach faithfully, to love deeply, and to pass on a living faith that endures beyond me. Let every word and every act of devotion become part of Your covenant story in my family."

How am I intentionally teaching faith in my home today? What everyday rhythms could become lessons of faith for the next generation?

DAY 29: FAITHFULNESS: MARKED BY COVENANT

A BIBLICAL WOMAN

DAY 30

Lydia

Wisdom: Discernment in Action

Lydia was a woman of means, intelligence, and spiritual depth. A seller of purple cloth in the bustling city of Philippi, she was both industrious and discerning. But beyond her business acumen, what set Lydia apart was her wisdom—rooted not in the world's ambition, but in a heart that listened for God's voice. When Paul began to preach by the riverside, the Lord opened her heart to receive the message, and she responded immediately with faith and hospitality.

Her home became one of the first churches in Europe, a gathering place for believers, missionaries, and seekers. Lydia knew how to use what she had for the Kingdom of God. She didn't wait for ideal conditions or for someone else to take the lead—her wisdom moved her to act. She understood that faith and stewardship walk hand in hand; that when God entrusts us with resources, influence, or knowledge, they are meant to be poured back into His work.

Lydia's story reminds every mother that wisdom is not simply knowing what is right, but doing it with grace. It's discerning when to speak and when to be silent, when to labor and when to rest, when to nurture and when to release. A wise mother doesn't just teach lessons—she embodies them, modeling godly priorities and quiet strength even when the world swirls with confusion.

Like Lydia, you are called to open your home, your heart, and your mind to the purposes of God. Wisdom often looks like small, steady faithfulness—listening to the Lord, shaping your family's rhythm around His Word, and creating a place where His Spirit can dwell freely. It is in these daily acts of understanding and obedience that the greatest legacies are formed.

DAY 30: WISDOM: DISCERNMENT IN ACTION

Reflection:

Ask God today for a heart like Lydia's—wise, responsive, and full of peace. How can you use what He has placed in your hands, your home, your gifts, your influence—to advance His Kingdom with wisdom and love?

Challenge:

Ask God for wisdom in one specific area of motherhood today. Then act in faith and obedience when He shows you the next step.

Deeper Study:

Proverbs 3:13–18 – Blessings of wisdom
    Acts 16:14–15 – Lydia's conversion
        Ephesians 1:17 – Spirit of wisdom

Prayer

LORD, *make my heart like Lydia's—open to Your truth, quick to obey, and wise in how I serve my family and You. Let every decision, every word, and every act of care reflect Your divine wisdom in me.*

Where in my home or heart do I most need the Spirit's wisdom right now? How might my family feel the fruit of that wisdom if I walk it out this week?

___

Day 30: Wisdom: Discernment in Action

A BIBLICAL WOMAN

DAY 31

Susanna

Sacrifice: Serving Quietly and Purely

Susanna is mentioned only briefly in Scripture, one of the women who followed Jesus, providing for Him out of their own means. "Joanna, the wife of Chuza, the manager of Herod's household; Susanna; and many others were helping to support them out of their own resources." Her name does not appear in the miracles, the debates, or the parables, but her quiet service speaks volumes. She represents every woman who has loved Jesus faithfully behind the scenes—without recognition, applause, or reward in this life.

Her sacrifice was not dramatic, but daily. She gave what she had: her time, her resources, her presence. She likely cooked, cleaned, and cared for the disciples on their journeys, turning ordinary service into sacred offering. While others sought position or visibility, Susanna sought only to follow her Savior wherever He went.

In a world that glorifies visibility, Susanna's hidden devotion is a holy rebuke. Jesus said, "Your Father, who sees what is done in secret, will reward you." Her life embodied that truth. The purest form of sacrifice is not measured by size but by sincerity.

Every unseen act of faithfulness, every prayer over a sleeping child, every meal made in love, every burden carried in silence—is noticed by God. The Kingdom advances not just through those who preach, but through those who quietly sustain the ones who do.

A mother's life often mirrors Susanna's, poured out in the quiet corners of home and heart. Her strength is steady, her love unshaken, her faith expressed in the small daily sacrifices that shape eternity. The Lord sees every unseen offering, and in His eyes, no labor of love is ever wasted.

Reflection:

Susanna's faith reminds us that quiet sacrifice is not weakness—it is worship. God measures devotion not by how much the world sees, but by how much the heart gives.

Challenge:

Offer an unseen act of service today purely for God's glory, expecting nothing in return. Let Matthew 10:42 remind you that even a cup of cold water, given in His name, will not go unrewarded.

Deeper Study:

Mark 15:40–41 – Women who followed Jesus
 Romans 12:1 – Living sacrifice
 Philippians 2:3–8 – Christ's humility

Prayer

LORD, teach me to serve like Susanna, with quiet purity, steadfast love, and a heart that gives without seeking recognition. May every hidden act of service reflect Your humility and draw others closer to You.

What small sacrifices am I making for my family or for God that I can begin to see as sacred? How might my unseen obedience become an act of worship this week?

Day 31: Sacrifice: Serving Quietly and Purely

A BIBLICAL WOMAN

DAY 32

Joanna

Sacrifice: Courageous Support

Joanna's story is one of quiet courage and unwavering strength. As the wife of Chuza, a high-ranking official in Herod's court, she lived within the very household that sought to destroy the Messiah she followed. Yet Joanna chose loyalty to Christ over comfort, risking her reputation, her safety, and her standing to stand with Him. "Where your treasure is, there your heart will be also."

Matthew 6:21

She not only followed Jesus but helped sustain His ministry through her own resources, turning her position of privilege into a platform of purpose. When others fled in fear, Joanna remained faithful. She stood near the cross and was among the first to arrive at the empty tomb, carrying spices to honor her crucified Lord. There she became one of the first witnesses of the resurrection, remembering the angel's words: "Why do you seek the living among the dead? He is not here, but has risen."

Luke 24:5–6

Joanna's life teaches us that true courage is often quiet but unyielding—the resolve to keep believing, serving, and standing for truth even when it costs everything. Strength isn't just about endurance, it's about steadfast faith in the storm, gentleness in leadership, and bravery in obedience.

Like Joanna, you are called to courageous support, to be the steady presence that holds faith firm in your home. Whether standing beside your husband, lifting up your children, or walking through trials alone, your quiet strength declares that Jesus is worthy of your trust, your resources, and your resolve.

DAY 32: SACRIFICE: COURAGEOUS SUPPORT

Reflection:

Joanna's courage flowed from quiet conviction. She teaches us that strength does not always roar—it often stands firm in faith when the world trembles. True sacrifice is not measured by loss, but by love that endures.

Challenge:

Strengthen someone's faith today with words of courage or an act of steadfast love. "Be on your guard; stand firm in the faith; be courageous; be strong." — 1 Corinthians 16:13

Deeper Study:

Luke 24:1–10 – Witness to the resurrection
    Proverbs 31:25 – Clothed in strength and dignity
    Psalm 18:32 – God makes me strong

Prayer

LORD, *make me strong like Joanna, faithful in adversity, courageous in obedience, and steadfast in serving Your Kingdom. Let my strength be quiet but unyielding, my love constant, and my devotion pure. May every act of courage point others back to You.*

Where is God asking me to stand firm rather than shrink back in fear? How can my faith anchor those around me?

Day 32: Sacrifice: Courageous Support

A BIBLICAL WOMAN

DAY 33

Joy: Faith That Won't Let Go

The Canaanite woman came to Jesus with desperation, but she left with joy. Her story begins in need and ends in triumph, revealing the kind of faith that refuses to let go, even when heaven seems silent. She was not from Israel, nor was she part of the chosen lineage, yet she recognized what many around Jesus could not: that He was Lord, the Son of David, and the only one who could heal her child.

When she cried out for mercy, Jesus at first appeared to ignore her. The disciples urged Him to send her away. Still, she persisted. Her love for her daughter and her belief in Jesus were stronger than her pride or her pain. Even when He tested her faith, saying, "It is not right to take the children's bread and toss it to the dogs," she replied humbly, "Yes, Lord, but even the dogs eat the crumbs that fall from their master's table."

Matthew 15:26–27

That moment broke through heaven's silence. Jesus answered her with joy and honor: "Woman, great is your faith! Let it be done for you as you desire." Matthew 15:28

Her daughter was healed instantly. Joy rushed in where sorrow had lived, and faith turned her trial into testimony.

The Canaanite woman teaches us that joy is not the absence of struggle; it is the reward of faith that endures through it. Her joy was born in persistence, humility, and trust. For every mother who has prayed for a child in distress, waited through silence, or felt unseen, her story reminds us that God's timing is not rejection. He delights in faith that presses closer when others give up.

Joy often comes when we stop demanding control and start trusting His heart. It's found in believing that even the crumbs of His goodness are enough to heal, redeem, and restore what we love most. Her faith became her song, and her joy, a living testimony that God honors those who cling to Him with unrelenting hope.

DAY 33: JOY: FAITH THAT WON'T LET GO

Reflection:

The Canaanite woman's joy came not from getting what she wanted, but from knowing the One who never turned her away. Her faith teaches us that even in silence, God is shaping the miracle, and joy is often the sound that follows surrender.

Challenge:

"Weeping may endure for a night, but joy comes in the morning." Psalm 30:5
Hold on to faith today in an area where you've grown weary, trusting that joy is already on its way.

Deeper Study:

Matthew 15:21–28 – The Canaanite woman's faith
Psalm 126:5–6 – Joy from tears
John 16:22 – Joy no one can take away

Prayer

LORD, give me the joy that clings to You in faith, believing that even when You seem silent, You are still good and still near. Let my hope endure, my heart trust, and my joy rise as proof of Your faithfulness.

Where have I seen joy spring up in places where I once felt hopeless? What has persistence in prayer taught me about God's faithfulness?

DAY 33: JOY: FAITH THAT WON'T LET GO

A BIBLICAL WOMAN

DAY 34

The Samaritan Woman

Respect: Reverence Through Transformation

The Samaritan woman came to the well at noon, carrying more than an empty jar, she carried shame, isolation, and the weight of her past. Yet it was there, in the heat of the day, that she met the living water Himself. Jesus saw her completely, her mistakes, her longings, her loneliness, and still chose to speak to her with compassion and truth. In that moment, respect was redefined.

He said to her, "Everyone who drinks this water will be thirsty again, but whoever drinks the water I give them will never thirst."

John 4:13–14 For the first time, someone looked at her not for what she had done, but for who she could become. Jesus didn't dismiss her story; He redeemed it. And in doing so, He restored her dignity.

The woman who once hid from others ran back into her town, declaring boldly, "Come, see a man who told me everything I ever did!"

John 4:29 The same voice that had once avoided the crowd now invited others to find the Savior. Her shame turned to testimony; her isolation became invitation.

The Samaritan woman's transformation teaches us that respect begins with seeing ourselves and others through God's eyes. True reverence flows from redemption—when we realize how deeply we've been forgiven, we learn to honor others with that same grace. Respect isn't earned through perfection; it's born from humility, gratitude, and the realization that we are loved beyond measure.

As mothers, wives, and daughters of God, respect begins in our hearts—how we speak, how we forgive, and how we treat those entrusted to our care. When we honor God in how we view others, our homes become places of peace and restoration—wells of living water for everyone who enters.

DAY 34: RESPECT: REVERENCE THROUGH TRANSFORMATION

Reflection:

The Samaritan woman reminds us that when Christ restores our identity, respect naturally follows—toward ourselves, others, and the One who redeemed us. True respect flows from grace received and grace given.

Challenge:

Speak words today that restore dignity—to yourself or to someone who has forgotten their worth in God's eyes. "Show proper respect to everyone; love the family of believers, fear God, honor the king." — 1 Peter 2:17

Deeper Study:

John 4:1–30 – Jesus and the woman at the well
    Isaiah 43:1 – Called by name
    Romans 12:10 – Honor one another

Prayer

LORD, thank You for seeing me when I was unseen and for restoring my worth. Teach me to extend that same respect and grace to others. May my words uplift, my actions honor, and my heart overflow with the dignity that comes from being Yours.

How has Jesus transformed the way I see myself—and how can I reflect that same grace toward others?

Day 34: Respect: Reverence Through Transformation

A BIBLICAL WOMAN

DAY 35

Mary Magdalene

Prayerfulness: Love That Clings to the Risen Lord

Mary Magdalene's story is one of profound transformation, from darkness to devotion, from torment to tender prayer. Once afflicted by seven demons, she experienced complete freedom through Jesus' healing touch. From that moment, her life became a living prayer, every act of service, every step she took, an offering of gratitude and love. She followed Him faithfully through His ministry, stood near the cross when others fled, and was the first to see the risen Christ.

Her prayerfulness wasn't confined to words, it was expressed in her presence. She lingered when others left. She sought Him in the garden, not to understand theology, but because her heart could not bear to be apart from Him. When the risen Lord spoke her name "Mary" she turned and cried out, "Rabboni!" (which means Teacher).

John 20:16

Her tears became prayers, her persistence became faith, and her devotion became the first proclamation of the resurrection: "I have seen the Lord."

John 20:18

Mary teaches us that prayer is more than speaking, it is staying. Staying when it's dark. Staying when it's quiet. Staying when you don't yet understand. The prayerful heart abides with Christ, trusting that even in confusion or grief, He is near. Her encounter at the tomb reveals that prayer opens our eyes to recognize Him where despair once blinded us.

A mother's prayer often mirrors Mary's, wordless, tear-stained, and fierce in love. God honors that kind of devotion. Prayerfulness is not the absence of activity; it's the posture of a heart continually turned toward Him. When we pray, we cling to the One who has already conquered the grave.

DAY 35: PRAYERFULNESS: LOVE THAT CLINGS TO THE RISEN LORD

Reflection:

Mary's story reminds us that prayer is not only asking, it is abiding. The soul that lingers with Jesus will always see resurrection. Prayer becomes love that stays when others leave, faith that endures until joy returns.

Challenge:

Set aside quiet moments today to simply linger in His presence, without agenda, just love and listen. "Pray without ceasing." — 1 Thessalonians 5:17

Deeper Study:

John 20:11–18 – Mary at the tomb
    Luke 8:1–3 – Women who followed Jesus
    Psalm 27:8 – Seek My face

Prayer

LORD, *make my heart like Mary's, faithful in sorrow, steadfast in love, and always lingering near Your presence in prayer. Teach me to stay when it's quiet, to trust when it's dark, and to cling to You until joy rises again.*

When have I felt closest to Jesus in prayer, and what drew me back to His presence? What might it look like to stay instead of strive?

DAY 35: PRAYERFULNESS: LOVE THAT CLINGS TO THE RISEN LORD

A BIBLICAL WOMAN

DAY 36

Jochebed

Faithfulness: Trusting God's Plan

Jochebed's faithfulness began in the shadows of fear. Pharaoh's decree demanded the death of every Hebrew son, yet she refused to surrender her child to despair. With courage born of trust, she hid baby Moses for three months, cradling a miracle in defiance of an empire. When she could hide him no longer, she built a small ark of reeds, sealed it with pitch, and placed her son in the Nile—entrusting her greatest treasure to the very river meant for his destruction.

This was not blind desperation—it was deliberate faith. Jochebed didn't abandon her son; she placed him in the hands of God. "By faith Moses was hidden by his parents for three months after his birth, because they saw that the child was beautiful, and they were not afraid of the king's edict." — Hebrews 11:23 Her faithfulness was active, creative, and courageous. And God honored it. The same river that could have claimed Moses' life carried him into Pharaoh's palace, where he would grow to deliver a nation. Faithfulness doesn't always look like control—it often looks like surrender.

For mothers, Jochebed's story speaks to the sacred act of release. Faithfulness is not clinging tighter—it's trusting deeper. It's teaching, nurturing, and then letting go, believing that the same God who called your children into existence will guide their path when you cannot.

Jochebed's legacy reminds us that faithfulness isn't proven in comfort but in crisis. Her story is a portrait of steadfast love anchored in divine confidence—a love that does what it can and entrusts the rest to God. The ark she wove with trembling hands became a vessel of providence, carrying not only her child, but the hope of a people.

DAY 36: FAITHFULNESS: TRUSTING GOD'S PLAN

Reflection:

Faithfulness is not the absence of fear, it's choosing trust in the midst of it. Jochebed shows us that surrender can be the strongest act of faith, especially when it comes to what we love most.

Challenge:

"Trust in the Lord with all your heart and lean not on your own understanding." — Proverbs 3:5 Choose one area where you're tempted to control, today, release it to God in prayer and peace.

Deeper Study:

Exodus 2:1–10 – Birth and rescue of Moses
    Hebrews 11:23 – Faith of Moses' parents
    Psalm 37:5 – Commit your way to the Lord

Prayer

LORD, give me Jochebed's faith—to do what I can, to trust what I can't, and to rest knowing You are faithful to complete what You began. Strengthen my heart to release what I love into Your care, and let my trust become testimony to Your unfailing plan.

What "basket" have I placed on the river of God's will, and can I trust Him with where it goes? How can I rest today knowing that His hands are stronger than my own?

DAY 36: FAITHFULNESS: TRUSTING GOD'S PLAN

A BIBLICAL WOMAN

DAY 37

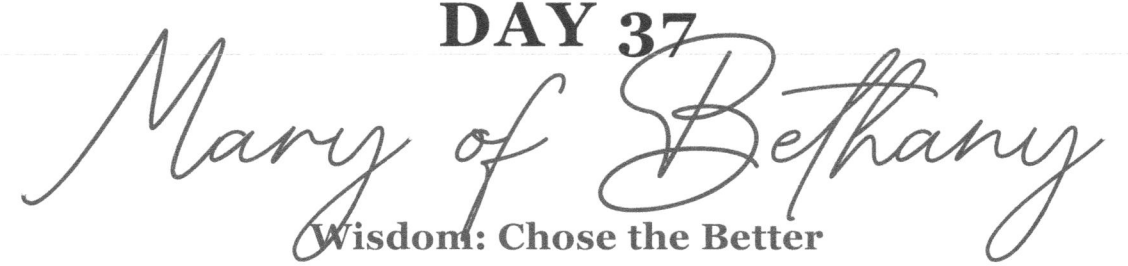

Mary of Bethany
Wisdom: Chose the Better

Mary of Bethany had a gift for recognizing what mattered most. While others bustled about with good intentions, she saw that wisdom begins not with effort, but with attention, attention fixed on the voice of Jesus. In a home filled with noise and preparation, she chose stillness. She sat at His feet, listening, learning, and loving the Lord with an undivided heart.

Her wisdom wasn't in doing more, it was in discerning when to stop. She understood that spiritual depth isn't found in constant motion, but in presence with God. When Martha voiced her frustration, Jesus gently answered, "Martha, Martha, you are anxious and troubled about many things, but one thing is necessary. Mary has chosen the good portion, which will not be taken away from her."

Luke 10:41–42

Later, at another meal, she would again act with insight that others missed. She anointed Jesus' feet with expensive perfume, wiping them with her hair, an act of devotion the disciples called wasteful, but He called beautiful. "Leave her alone," Jesus said. "She has done a beautiful thing to Me."

Mark 14:6

Her wisdom came from knowing Him personally, not merely knowing about Him. True wisdom flows from intimacy, and intimacy requires time at His feet.

As mothers, leaders, and disciples, we often carry Martha's burden of busyness. Yet Mary reminds us that wisdom begins in worship. It's not found in multitasking faith, but in singular focus, choosing the better part. To listen before leading, to sit before serving, to rest before rushing. Those who live in His presence will know what to do when the moment calls for action.

DAY 37: WISDOM: CHOSE THE BETTER

Reflection:

Wisdom isn't just knowledge, it's knowing when to pause and who to listen to. Mary's stillness before Jesus was her greatest act of discernment, teaching us that presence always precedes purpose.

Challenge:

"The fear of the Lord is the beginning of wisdom." — Proverbs 9:10
Set aside time today for quiet prayer or Scripture reading, no agenda, no rush. Just sit with Jesus and listen.

Deeper Study:

Luke 10:38–42 – Mary and Martha
John 12:1–8 – Anointing at Bethany
Colossians 3:16 – Let the Word dwell richly

Prayer

LORD, teach me the wisdom of Mary, to quiet my heart, to sit at Your feet, and to choose the better part that will never be taken away. In stillness, give me discernment; in presence, grant me peace; and in every season, remind me that wisdom begins with You.

When was the last time I chose presence with God over productivity for God, and what fruit came from that moment? How can I create space daily to listen before I act?

DAY 37: WISDOM: CHOSE THE BETTER

A BIBLICAL WOMAN

DAY 38

Virtue

Dorcas was known not for her words, but for her works. Her life was a tapestry of kindness, stitched together one act of love at a time. In the seaside town of Joppa, her hands became instruments of compassion. She sewed garments for widows, cared for the poor, and gave freely without expectation. Her sacrifice was woven into fabric and friendship alike, and her community flourished because of it.

Scripture says, "She was always doing good and helping the poor."
Acts 9:36

When Dorcas died, her absence was felt deeply. The widows she had clothed gathered around her body, weeping and holding up the garments she had made for them. Their tears were testimony: this woman had lived her faith. Her love was tangible.

So powerful was her legacy of giving that God, through Peter, restored her to life, making her story a living parable of how generosity multiplies resurrection. Peter prayed, then said, "Tabitha, arise." She opened her eyes, and when she saw him, she sat up.
Acts 9:40

True sacrifice often looks ordinary. It's the mother mending what others overlook, the friend who listens without rush, the believer who gives without being asked. Dorcas teaches us that when love takes the shape of service, the smallest offerings become holy. The garments she crafted became more than clothing, they became coverings of dignity and reminders of God's care.

In every generation, God uses quiet servants like Dorcas to keep His compassion visible in the world. Each act of sacrifice is a seed that outlives the giver. Every thread of love, woven in prayer, patience, and perseverance, becomes a garment of grace that wraps another soul in warmth.

DAY 38: WISDOM: CHOSE THE BETTER

Reflection:

Dorcas reminds us that sacrificial love doesn't need a stage, it needs willing hands. Every unseen act of service stitches hope into someone's story and leaves the fragrance of Christ behind.

Challenge:

"Do not forget to do good and to share with others, for with such sacrifices God is pleased." — Hebrews 13:16. Use your hands today to bless someone tangibly, a meal, a note, a gift, or a quiet act of help given in love.

Deeper Study:

Acts 9:36–42 – Dorcas restored to life
    Galatians 6:9–10 – Do good to all people
    Philippians 2:3–4 – Consider others first

Prayer

LORD, may my hands like Dorcas's, serve with joy, give with grace, and bless others in ways that reflect Your heart. Help me see every task as a holy act of love, and every act of love as worship to You.

How can I turn my daily routines into sacred acts of service that reflect God's love? In what ways can my hands become instruments of healing, comfort, or blessing today?

DAY 38: WISDOM: CHOSE THE BETTER

DAY 39
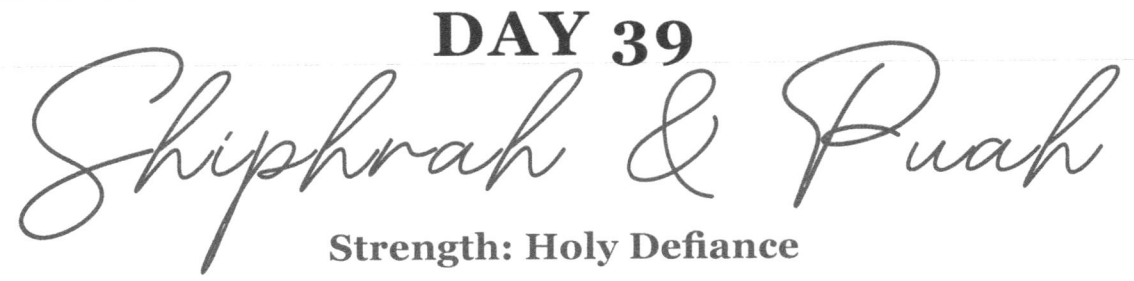
Shiphrah & Puah
Strength: Holy Defiance

Long before Moses lifted his staff or Pharaoh's army was drowned in the sea, two women quietly changed the course of history. Shiphrah and Puah were Hebrew midwives living under Pharaoh's ruthless decree to kill every newborn Hebrew boy. They had no armies, no political power, and no allies in high places, yet they possessed something far stronger: the fear of God.

When Pharaoh ordered them to commit murder in the name of empire, they refused. "But the midwives feared God and did not do as the king of Egypt commanded them, but saved the male children alive."

Exodus 1:17

Their courage was not loud or violent; it was holy and steadfast. They risked their lives to protect innocent children, and Scripture says, "God dealt well with the midwives, and the people multiplied and grew very strong."

Exodus 1:20

These two women, standing firm in faith, became the first recorded resistance to Pharaoh's tyranny, and through them, the deliverer of Israel would one day be born. Strength, as Shiphrah and Puah reveal, is not measured in muscle or might, it's measured in moral courage. True strength is doing what is right even when the cost is great.

It is the mother who shields her child, the believer who speaks truth in love, the servant who honors God above man. Their story reminds us that quiet obedience in the face of evil shakes the foundations of kingdoms. Every generation needs women like them, women of holy defiance who refuse to bow to fear or compromise.

Strength is not about dominance but devotion, not defiance for its own sake, but for righteousness' sake. The world changes when godly women stand their ground, even if their names are known only to Heaven.

DAY 39: STRENGTH: HOLY DEFIANCE

Reflection:

Shiphrah and Puah show that true strength is found in revering God more than man. Fear fades where holy conviction stands firm, and courage becomes worship when it defends what is sacred.

Challenge:

"Be strong and courageous; do not be afraid… for the Lord your God is with you wherever you go." — Joshua 1:9
Stand firm in one area where the world's voice conflicts with God's Word—honor Him with your courage today.

Deeper Study:

Exodus 1:15–21 – The midwives' courage
Psalm 27:1 – The Lord is my strength
Ephesians 6:10–13 – Put on the armor of God

Prayer

LORD, make me strong like Shiphrah and Puah, to stand in holy defiance against evil and to fear You more than anything else. Give me courage to obey when it costs, and faith to trust that Your strength is made perfect in my weakness.

Where is God calling me to take a courageous stand in faith, even if it means standing alone? What promise from His Word strengthens me to obey despite fear?

DAY 39: STRENGTH: HOLY DEFIANCE

A BIBLICAL WOMAN

DAY 40

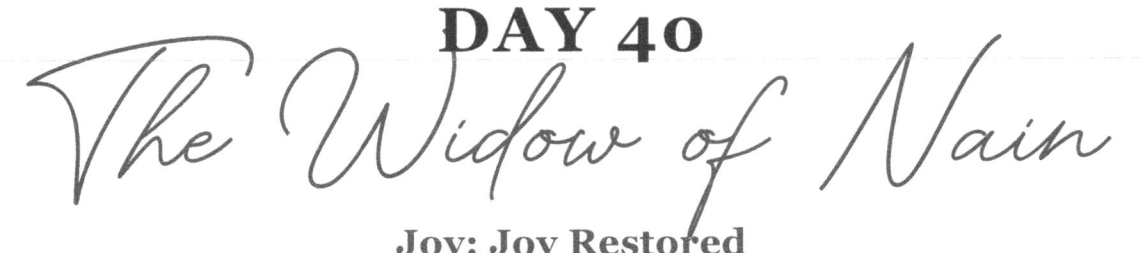

Joy: Joy Restored

The Widow of Nain was walking in a funeral procession when she met Life Himself. Her only son was gone, the last remnant of her family and her hope. As the mourners carried the boy's body out of the city gate, grief consumed her steps. Yet in that moment, Jesus met her on the road between despair and destiny. His compassion stirred, and with one touch, sorrow turned to song.

When the Lord saw her, "His heart went out to her and He said,
'Do not weep.'" Then He touched the bier and spoke into death itself: "Young man, I say to you, arise."
Luke 7:13–14

And he did. The boy sat up and began to speak, and Jesus gave him back to his mother.
It is one of the most tender miracles in Scripture, not a request made, but compassion initiated. God moved because His heart broke for her pain.

Joy, for the believer, often begins where we least expect it. It is not the denial of sorrow, but the redemption of it. The Widow of Nain teaches us that God sees the weeping mother, the empty arms, the heart that can't hold another loss. And He still moves with mercy. His compassion restores joy to those who thought it was gone forever.

Her story reminds us that joy is not something we create, it's something God restores. Even when hope feels buried, He can speak life into what seems beyond recovery. The same Jesus who stopped a funeral in Nain still interrupts sorrow today.

Reflection:

Joy is not found in what we keep, but in Who gives back what was lost. The Lord still turns mourning into dancing, proving that no grief is beyond His reach.

Challenge:

"Those who sow in tears shall reap in joy." — Psalm 126:5
   Bring your sorrow to Jesus in prayer today, ask Him to breathe new life into the place where joy once lived.

Deeper Study:

Luke 7:11–17 – The widow's son raised
   Psalm 30:11 – You turned my mourning into dancing
   Isaiah 61:3 – Beauty for ashes

Prayer

LORD, *thank You for seeing my sorrow; speak life into my heart again and restore the joy that only You can give. Let my tears water the soil where new hope will grow, and may my story sing of Your compassion and power.*

What loss or disappointment do I need to place back into the hands of God so that He can restore joy? How might He already be working to bring beauty from my ashes?

Day 40: Joy: Joy Restored

A Biblical Woman

DAY 41

Hagar

Respect: The God Who Sees

Hagar's story is one of pain and profound encounter. A servant in Sarah's household, she became pregnant with Abraham's son at Sarah's request—only to be mistreated and cast out when jealousy took root. Alone and afraid in the wilderness, Hagar fled with nothing but the child in her womb and the ache of rejection in her heart. Yet it was there, in her lowest place, that God met her.

"The angel of the Lord found her by a spring of water in the wilderness… and said, 'Hagar, servant of Sarai, where have you come from and where are you going?'"
Genesis 16:7–8

He promised her descendants too numerous to count and named her son Ishmael—"God hears." Overwhelmed by divine mercy, Hagar gave God a new name in return: "You are the God who sees me."
Genesis 16:13

She, an Egyptian slave, became the first person in Scripture to give God a name. Respect, at its root, means "to see again." In Hagar's encounter, we learn that God's respect for humanity flows from His sight, He sees every story, every sorrow, every injustice. And when we know that we are seen and valued by Him, we can extend that same respect to others. Hagar's dignity was not restored by her circumstances, but by God's gaze.

For every woman who has felt invisible or dismissed, Hagar's story whispers truth: You are not forgotten. The God who saw her by the spring still sees you where you are. Respect begins in receiving His gaze with gratitude, knowing you are fully known and deeply loved. From that sacred assurance flows the strength to treat others with the same honor and compassion.

DAY 41: RESPECT: THE GOD WHO SEES

Reflection:

Respect begins when we remember that God sees every life as precious. Like Hagar, we are restored when we recognize His gaze upon us and reflect that same dignity toward others.

Challenge:

"You are the God who sees me." — Genesis 16:13
  Look intentionally at someone who feels unseen today—speak kindness, show patience, or serve them with compassion that mirrors God's heart.

Deeper Study:

Genesis 16:1–16 – Hagar and Ishmael's promise
  Psalm 139:1–12 – You see me always
  Luke 12:6–7 – You are of great value

Prayer

LORD, *thank You for being the God who sees me. When I feel forgotten, remind me that Your eyes never leave me. Help me reflect that same respect and compassion toward others who need to be reminded of their worth in You.*

When have I felt truly seen by God, and how did it change my confidence or compassion toward others? How can I make someone else feel seen this week?

Day 41: Respect: The God Who Sees

A BIBLICAL WOMAN

DAY 42

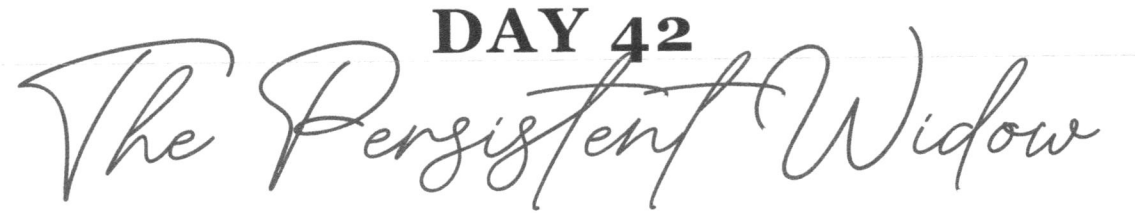

The Persistent Widow

Prayerfulness: Keep Knocking

The Persistent Widow is one of Jesus' most powerful parables of prayer. She had no status, no husband, and no advocate, but she had determination. Every day she came before an unjust judge, pleading for justice against her adversary. The judge ignored her, delayed her, and dismissed her, but she kept coming. Her persistence eventually wore down his resistance. "Because this widow keeps bothering me, I will see that she gets justice," he said.

Luke 18:5

Jesus told this story so that His followers would "always pray and not give up." Her faith was her voice, and her voice was her weapon. The world might have called her powerless, but Heaven called her unstoppable. Prayer, Jesus revealed, isn't about eloquence; it's about endurance. The faithful heart keeps knocking, not because God is hard to persuade, but because perseverance transforms the one who prays.

For every mother who has prayed over a child's future, every believer who has interceded for a wandering loved one, or every heart still waiting for breakthrough, the Persistent Widow's story says, don't stop now. God hears the prayers that refuse to quit. Persistent prayer refines faith, strengthens trust, and aligns the heart with God's will.

Prayerfulness is not passivity, it's holy pursuit. The widow's unrelenting petitions reveal that prayer is not about convincing God, but about clinging to Him until His perfect timing unfolds. Her persistence became a sermon Jesus still preaches through every praying heart: keep praying, keep trusting, keep knocking.

DAY 42: PRAYERFULNESS: KEEP KNOCKING

Reflection:

Prayerfulness is persistence in the presence of God. It's faith that refuses to let go until Heaven answers, and in the waiting, we are changed.

Challenge:

"Ask, and it will be given to you; seek, and you will find; knock, and it will be opened to you." — Matthew 7:7   Return to one prayer you've grown tired of repeating—and pray it again today with renewed faith.

Deeper Study:

Luke 18:1–8 – The Persistent Widow
    James 5:16–18 – The power of fervent prayer
    Romans 12:12 – Faithful in prayer

Prayer

LORD, *give me the heart of the Persistent Widow, to pray with endurance, to trust with confidence, and to keep knocking until Your perfect will unfolds. Teach me to persevere not out of fear, but out of faith that You are always listening.*

What promise or person have I stopped praying for, and how can I re-engage in faithful, expectant prayer? What might God be shaping in me through persistence?

DAY 42: PRAYERFULNESS: KEEP KNOCKING

A BIBLICAL WOMAN

DAY
The Widow of Zarephath

Faithfulness: Steadfast in Scarcity

The Widow of Zarephath lived at the edge of survival. With famine spreading across the land, her pantry was down to one handful of flour and a few drops of oil. She had resigned herself to bake a final loaf for her son and herself before dying. But that day, God sent a prophet to her door. Elijah asked her for water—and then for bread. It was a request that tested her heart and her faith.

Elijah said to her, "Do not be afraid; go and do as you have said. But first make me a little cake of it and bring it to me… for thus says the Lord, the God of Israel: 'The jar of flour shall not be spent, and the jug of oil shall not be empty.'" — 1 Kings 17:13–14 With trembling hands, she gave what little she had, trusting that God's word was true. And as she poured out the oil and measured the flour, she found that it never ran out. Each day, just enough. Each morning, another provision. Her faithfulness in lack became the stage for God's abundance.

Faithfulness often shows its strength when resources run thin. This widow teaches us that trust in God is not proven in plenty but in the willingness to give when nothing seems left. It's faith that clings to His promise when the jar looks empty. Every act of obedience, however small, becomes a declaration: "I believe He will provide."

As mothers and believers, we often stand at our own jars of flour and oil—time, energy, hope, or means stretched to the limit. Yet when we offer what we have to God, He multiplies it. Faithfulness in scarcity builds the kind of endurance that keeps believing even when the world says, "It's over."

DAY 42: FAITHFULNESS: STEADFAST IN SCARCITY

Reflection:

Faithfulness is trusting God with your last handful and believing His word will sustain you through the famine. True faith gives first and fears later, because it knows who the Provider is.

Challenge:

"And my God will supply every need of yours according to His riches in glory in Christ Jesus." — Philippians 4:19   Give or serve in one area today where it costs something, your time, your comfort, or your convenience, and watch how God provides.

Deeper Study:

1 Kings 17:7–16 – Elijah and the widow's faith
2 Corinthians 9:8 – God's abundant provision
Matthew 6:31–33 – Seek first His kingdom

Prayer

LORD, teach me to trust You like the widow of Zarephath—to give faithfully, believe fully, and live expecting Your daily provision. Let my small offerings become a testimony of Your endless supply.

What "jar" in my life feels nearly empty, and how might God be inviting me to trust Him with it? How can I live as though His promises are already true?

DAY 42: FAITHFULNESS: STEADFAST IN SCARCITY

A Biblical Woman

DAY 44

Virtue

The Proverbs 31 woman is often described as the picture of perfection, but her story is not about flawlessness. It's about faithful wisdom lived out in the rhythm of daily life. She rises early, works diligently, manages her home, nurtures her family, and invests her energy in what brings life and goodness. Her wisdom is not lofty or distant, it's practical, productive, and profoundly spiritual.

She understands that true wisdom begins with reverence for the Lord: "Charm is deceptive, and beauty is fleeting; but a woman who fears the Lord is to be praised." Proverbs 31:30

Every decision she makes, every word she speaks, flows from a heart anchored in His truth. Her strength and dignity do not come from her achievements but from her alignment with God's order. She is not driven by comparison or fear, she walks in purpose. Her home flourishes because she builds it with discernment and love.

The Proverbs 31 woman teaches us that wisdom is not confined to study, it is lived out through stewardship. It's knowing when to speak and when to listen, when to labor and when to rest, when to lead and when to follow. Her example reminds mothers and women of every season that the holy work of home, service, and influence is sacred ground. God's wisdom shines brightest when lived humbly and consistently.

Her husband trusts her, her children bless her, and her community respects her, not because she's extraordinary, but because she's faithful in the ordinary. The fruit of wisdom is peace, and the Proverbs 31 woman walks in it daily. She shows us that when God's Word shapes our ways, every task becomes worship.

DAY 44: FAITHFULNESS: STEADFAST IN SCARCITY

Reflection:

Wisdom is not measured by knowledge but by fruit, peace, diligence, and love rooted in reverence for God. When our daily routines are guided by His wisdom, our homes become reflections of His heart.

Challenge:

"The fear of the Lord is the beginning of wisdom." — Proverbs 9:10
Choose one daily routine, like cooking, cleaning, or planning, and turn it into a moment of worship and intentional wisdom.

Deeper Study:

How can I bring God's wisdom into the ordinary moments of my day so that they become extraordinary in meaning? What area of my home or heart needs the peace that comes from wise stewardship?

Prayer

LORD, *give me the wisdom of the Proverbs 31 woman—to build with purpose, to speak with grace, and to walk each day in reverent strength. Let my home, my words, and my work reflect Your wisdom in all things.*

How can I bring God's wisdom into the ordinary moments of my day so that they become extraordinary in meaning? What area of my home or heart needs the peace that comes from wise stewardship?

Day 44: Faithfulness: Steadfast in Scarcity

A BIBLICAL WOMAN

DAY 45

Zipporah
Sacrifice: Covenant Obedience

Night fell over the desert road as Moses journeyed back to Egypt, carrying the call of God but not yet the full obedience of it. The Lord had chosen him to deliver Israel, yet a vital command of the covenant had been left undone; his own son remained uncircumcised. On that lonely road, judgment drew near, and the life of the child hung in the balance.

In that moment of crisis, it was Zipporah, Moses' Midianite wife, who acted swiftly and faithfully. She understood what Moses hesitated to do. Taking a flint knife, she circumcised her son and touched the blood to Moses, saying, "Surely you are a bridegroom of blood to me."

Exodus 4:25

Through her decisive obedience, the wrath of God was turned away, and His covenant mercy was renewed over their family.

Zipporah's act was not one of rebellion but of reverence. She did what was hard and holy because she valued God's covenant above her comfort. Her sacrifice was both physical and spiritual—a moment of costly obedience that preserved the deliverer of Israel and secured God's purpose for generations to come.

Her story reminds us that sacrifice and obedience are inseparable. Sometimes, God calls us to act when others hesitate, to make a difficult decision that restores alignment between our household and His Word. Covenant obedience may cost something in the moment, but it clears the path for blessing and divine protection to flow again.

For every mother, wife, and believer standing between promise and fulfillment, Zipporah's faithfulness whispers courage: when God's covenant calls, obedience cannot wait.

DAY 45: SACRIFICE: COVENANT OBEDIENCE

Reflection:

Zipporah's story shows that sacrifice and obedience are often inseparable. God honors the heart that acts in alignment with His covenant, even when others hesitate.

Challenge:

"To obey is better than sacrifice, and to heed is better than the fat of rams."
— 1 Samuel 15:22   Obey promptly today in one area God has been prompting you, trust that even hard obedience brings His covering and blessing.

Deeper Study:

Exodus 4:18–26 – Zipporah's decisive act
    Genesis 17:9–14 – The covenant of circumcision
    Romans 12:1 – A living sacrifice

Prayer

LORD, *give me Zipporah's courage to act in covenant obedience, swiftly, faithfully, and without hesitation, so that Your purposes can move forward through my life.*

Is there an area in my life where delayed obedience is holding back God's work? What step can I take today to bring my actions into full alignment with His will?

Day 45: Sacrifice: Covenant Obedience

A Biblical Woman

SCRIPTURE REFERENCE GUIDE

FAITHFULNESS
Rooted in loyalty, covenant devotion, and steadfast trust.
Ruth 1:16–17
Lamentations 3:22–23
Psalm 37:3–6
Joshua 2:8–11
Joshua 2:9, 11
Hebrews 10:23
Hebrews 11:31
James 2:25
Ruth 1:16–17 (Naomi's legacy)
Psalm 119:90
2 Timothy 1:5
2 Kings 4:18–37
Hebrews 11:35
Psalm 112:7

WISDOM
Guided truth, discernment, and the radiance of understanding.
1 Samuel 25:24
1 Samuel 25:32–33
Proverbs 18:21
Proverbs 6:23
Proverbs 9:10
Proverbs 25:11
Proverbs 2:6
Proverbs 31:26
James 1:5
James 1:19–20
Colossians 3:16
Colossians 4:5
Colossians 4:6
2 Kings 22:16, 19–20
Acts 18:24–26

SERVICE / SACRIFICE
Hidden holiness, humility, and giving what costs something.
John 13:8
John 13:15
Mark 9:35
Colossians 3:23–24
Galatians 5:13
1 Kings 17:8–16
1 Kings 17:12
Luke 21:1–4
Romans 12:1
Esther 4:14
Psalm 27:1
2 Timothy 1:7
Joshua 1:9
2 Kings 11:2–3
John 15:13
Philippians 2:4
Romans 12:1 (repeated emphasis)
Song of Solomon 8:7
Matthew 5:4
2 Samuel 21:10
Romans 12:12
Galatians 6:9

STRENGTH

Obedience, courage, and endurance clothed in dignity.

Judges 4:14
Joshua 1:9
Isaiah 40:29–31
2 Corinthians 12:9–10
Nehemiah 8:10
Psalm 18:32
2 Corinthians 12:9
Exodus 2:6
Proverbs 31:8
Exodus 2:5–10
Psalm 82:3
Isaiah 1:17

JOY

Gratitude, rejoicing, and the strength that comes from gladness.

Luke 1:42
Luke 1:46–47
John 15:11
Romans 12:12
Psalm 16:11
Genesis 21:6
Genesis 21:1–7
Habakkuk 3:17–19
Philippians 4:4
Exodus 15:21
Psalm 30:11
Habakkuk 3:18
Psalm 126:5
Luke 7:13–14
Luke 7:11–17
Isaiah 61:3

RESPECT

Strength under order, reverence that builds unity.

1 Peter 3:6
Ephesians 5:33
1 Peter 3:1–4
Proverbs 14:1
Genesis 24:67
Genesis 24:15–20
Romans 12:10
Philippians 2:3
Romans 16:1–2
1 Peter 2:17

PRAYERFULNESS

Intimacy with God through perseverance and surrender.

1 Samuel 1:11
1 Samuel 1:15
1 Samuel 2:1
Philippians 4:6–7
1 Samuel 1:10–20
Ephesians 6:18
Luke 2:38
Luke 2:36–38
1 Thessalonians 5:17
Colossians 4:2
Luke 1:46–55
Philippians 4:6
1 Thessalonians 5:16–18

Scripture reference guide: Sacrifice: Covenant Obedience

The Crown of Womanhood

A Reflection And Prayer of Blessing

Over these forty-five days, we have walked beside women whose stories were etched by the hand of God—some celebrated, others unnamed—but all remembered by Heaven. Their lives whisper one unshakable truth: the heart of a woman, surrendered to God, is one of His most powerful instruments for redemption. They remind us that holiness is not confined to pulpits or palaces—it flourishes in kitchens and classrooms, in boardrooms and battlefields, in hospital rooms and hidden corners of prayer. Whether leading a nation or nurturing a child, every woman who yields her life to the Lord becomes a vessel of eternal influence.
The seven virtues we've studied—Faithfulness, Wisdom, Sacrifice, Strength, Joy, Respect, and Prayerfulness—form the radiant rhythm of a God-centered life. They are not medals to earn, but graces to receive. They are not burdens to bear, but blessings to cultivate:

Faithfulness steadies our steps when the road is uncertain.
Wisdom teaches us when to speak and when to be still.
Sacrifice reveals that love always costs something—and is always worth it.
Strength reminds us that courage need not roar; it can simply stand.
Joy transforms hardship into holy hope.
Respect restores dignity—to others and to ourselves.
Prayerfulness keeps us near the heart of God, the source of all peace.

Together, these virtues form a crown—a sacred emblem of divine womanhood. The world may define women by beauty, performance, or applause, but God defines her by abiding: by a faithful heart, a discerning mind, and a spirit anchored in His love.
You were made for this kind of life—the kind that walks in peace when others panic, that heals with words, builds with wisdom, and believes when the world forgets how. The Crown of Womanhood is not worn for recognition, but for reflection—so that when the world looks at you, it sees Him.

our Final Reflection

You have journeyed through forty-five days of women whose lives tell God's truth in a thousand different ways.
 Their seasons mirror our own: faith and failure, pain and promise, struggle and song.
 Each story was a mirror of grace, reminding us that God still writes redemption through willing hearts.
Let their lives whisper to yours: you are part of that same legacy.
 Walk forward wearing your crown, not as a symbol of achievement, but as a reflection of grace.
 You are not defined by what you've lost, by what the world expects, or by what others see.
 You are defined by the One who calls you beloved.
Hold your head high, daughter of God.
 The virtues you've studied, faithfulness, wisdom, sacrifice, strength, joy, respect, and prayerfulness, are not distant ideals, but living gifts within you.
 Carry them into your home, your work, your relationships, and your worship.
 Let your life shine as proof that holiness still walks among us, quiet, steadfast, and crowned with grace.

www.ingramcontent.com/pod-product-compliance
Lightning Source LLC
Chambersburg PA
CBHW051325110526
44582CB00004B/99